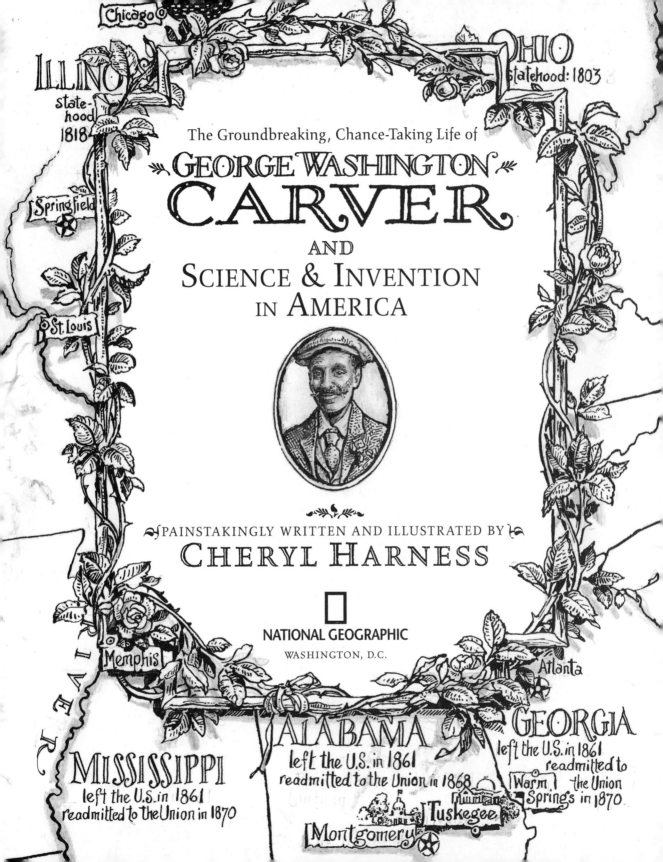

The Groundbreaking, Chance-Taking Life of

GEORGE WASHINGTON
CARVER

AND
SCIENCE & INVENTION
IN AMERICA

PAINSTAKINGLY WRITTEN AND ILLUSTRATED BY

CHERYL HARNESS

NATIONAL GEOGRAPHIC

WASHINGTON, D.C.

CHICAGO

ILLINOIS
statehood 1818

Springfield

St. Louis

OHIO
statehood: 1803

MISSISSIPPI RIVER

Memphis

MISSISSIPPI
left the U.S. in 1861
readmitted to the Union in 1870

ALABAMA
left the U.S. in 1861
readmitted to the Union in 1868

Montgomery

Tuskegee

GEORGIA
left the U.S. in 1861
readmitted to the Union in 1870

Warm
Springs

Atlanta

"Speak to the earth and it shall teach thee."

— Bible, Job 12:7

"Science without religion is lame.
Religion without science is blind."

— Albert Einstein

"The study of nature is not only entertaining,
but instructive and the only true method
that leads up to the development of a
creative mind and a clear understanding
of the great natural principles."

— GWC, February 24, 1930

Contents

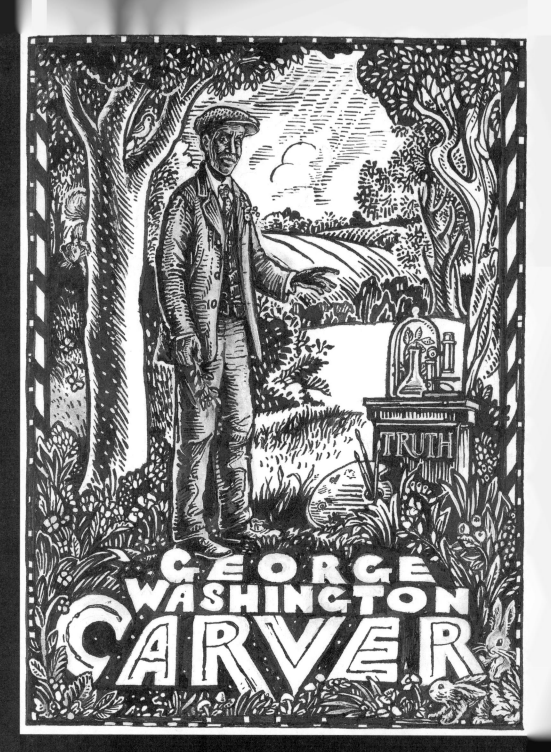

GEORGE WASHINGTON CARVER

SOMETIME AROUND THE END OF THE AMERICAN CIVIL WAR, a peaceful man was born into a violent world. Here in the future, we know little about his mother, Mary, beyond the facts that she called her child George, and they, being enslaved, carried the last name of their white owner. As a young man, George gave himself a middle name, that of a hero who began a nation based upon liberty. George Washington Carver, who became something of a hero himself, lived out his long life in an astonishing age of invention, epic wars, industrial growth, and cruel racism. It meant that, despite his talent and brilliance, he had to struggle for an education, the key that would unlock doors shut in his dark-skinned face. The dramatic story of his life, the obstacles he overcame, his twin quests for knowledge and respect, plus folks' fascination with what they thought they knew about the "Sage of Tuskegee" — all of these made George Washington Carver an American hero then and now.

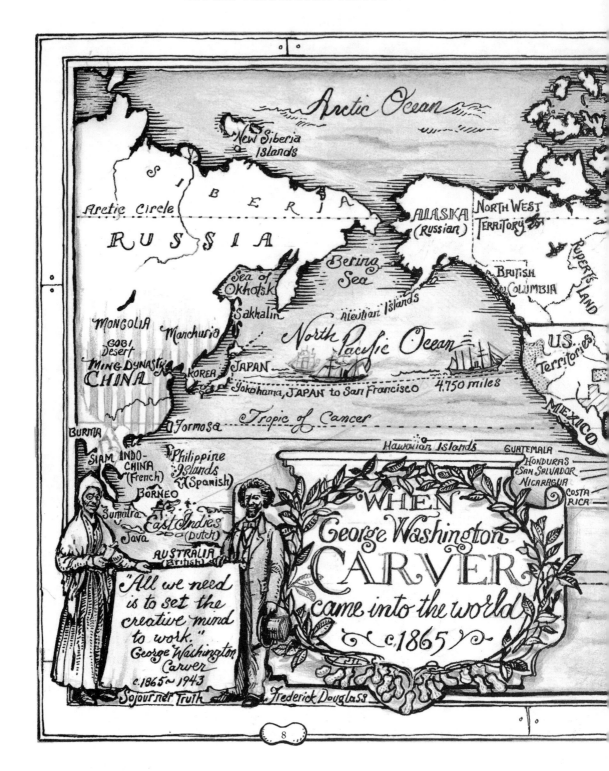

Arctic Ocean

New Siberia Islands

SIBERIA

Arctic Circle

RUSSIA

ALASKA (Russian)

NORTH WEST TERRITORY

RUPERT'S LAND

Bering Sea

BRITISH COLUMBIA

Sea of Okhotsk

Sakhalin

Aleutian Islands

MONGOLIA

GOBI Desert

Manchuria

North Pacific Ocean

U.S. Territories

MING DYNASTY CHINA

KOREA

JAPAN

MEXICO

Yokohama, JAPAN to San Francisco   4,750 miles

Formosa

Tropic of Cancer

Hawaiian Islands

GUATEMALA

BURMA

SIAM INDO-CHINA (French)

Philippine Islands (Spanish)

HONDURAS
SAN SALVADOR
NICARAGUA

BORNEO

COSTA RICA

Sumatra

East Indies (Dutch)

Java

AUSTRALIA British

"All we need
is to set the
creative mind
to work."
George Washington
Carver
c.1865 ~ 1943

Sojourner Truth

WHEN
George Washington
CARVER
came into the world
c.1865

Frederick Douglass

CHAPTER ONE

AN INORDINATE DESIRE FOR KNOWLEDGE

MARY OF DIAMOND GROVE

MOSES CARVER AND HIS WIFE SUSAN were kindly, independent folks. They didn't approve of slavery, but it was legal in Missouri, and farming was hard work. They had no children to help, and, after all, it wasn't so easy to hire folks out in the backcountry. So, in 1855, the Carvers paid $700 (approximately $16,000 in today's money) to a neighbor in exchange for 13-year-old Mary and a written guarantee that she was "sound in body and mind and a slave for life."

Mary settled in at the Carvers' farm, near the frontier hamlet of Diamond Grove. Moses and Susan put her to work at the

---

1864 Note: The time line features events that took place around the world during George Washington Carver's lifetime.

Louis Pasteur *invents pasteurization.*

Nov. 8 — The U.S. conducts a national election in the middle of a civil war: pretty amazing! **Abraham Lincoln** *is reelected.*

Nov. 16 – Dec. 20 — U.S. **General William T. Sherman**'s *Yankee soldiers rumble through Georgia on their march from Atlanta to Savannah.*

SHERMAN

Science fiction writer **Jules Verne** *publishes* A Journey to the Center of the Earth.

spinning wheel, over the stove and washtubs, and in the garden. She helped to look after cows, pigs, chickens, and, in time, her children, perhaps five in all. There might have been a pair of baby girls who died. As for their father(s), little is known. Moses recorded that Mary's son Jim was born October 10, 1859. As for Jim's little brother, there is no exact birthday. What we do know for sure is that violence swirled around the time-space intersection at which George Washington Carver came into the world.

Jim helps his mother with the chores.

1865

Pulaski, TN — Confederate Army veterans call their new social club the Ku Klux Klan. The KKK will be outlawed in 1871 (see 1915).

Glasgow, Scotland — Surgery will be less germy and deadly thanks to **Dr. Joseph Lister,** who pioneers the use of carbolic acid as an antiseptic.

April 14 – 15 — Washington, DC — **President Abraham Lincoln** is shot and mortally wounded by actor/assassin **John Wilkes Booth. Vice President Andrew Johnson** becomes the 17th U.S. President.

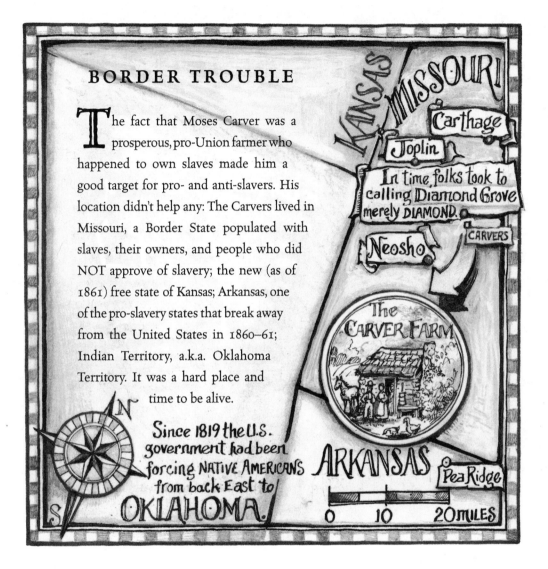

BORDER TROUBLE

The fact that Moses Carver was a prosperous, pro-Union farmer who happened to own slaves made him a good target for pro- and anti-slavers. His location didn't help any: The Carvers lived in Missouri, a Border State populated with slaves, their owners, and people who did NOT approve of slavery; the new (as of 1861) free state of Kansas; Arkansas, one of the pro-slavery states that break away from the United States in 1860–61; Indian Territory, a.k.a. Oklahoma Territory. It was a hard place and time to be alive.

Since 1819 the U.S. government had been forcing NATIVE AMERICANS from back East to OKLAHOMA.

KANSAS

MISSOURI

Carthage

Joplin

In time, folks took to calling Diamond Grove merely DIAMOND.

CARVERS

Neosho

The CARVER FARM

ARKANSAS

Pea Ridge

0 10 20 MILES

N
S

1865

April 27 —
Mississippi River —
The boilers blow up
on the steamboat
Sultana, killing
more than
1,500 people.

May 26 —
The American
Civil War is
officially over.

Dec. 6 —
The 13th Amendment makes
slavery illegal in the U.S.,
which is trying to patch things
up with the ruined states of
the defeated Confederacy.
This long, rocky road is called
Reconstruction (see 1876).

13

A HARD BEGINNING IN A HARSH PLACE

GEORGE WOULD WRITE YEARS LATER that he was born "about 2 weeks before the war closed." He meant the Civil War between the United States and the breakaway, slaveholding Confederate States of America (C.S.A.). It ended in April 1865. This was right about the time that George's father, a slave from a nearby farm, died in an accident when he and a team of oxen were hauling wood. Fate had more tragedy in store. Baby George, his sister, and his mother were grabbed by outlaws and carried off to Arkansas.

Raids like this had been going on since the mid-1850s when the nation's long argument over slavery zeroed in on the question of whether or not the practice would spread into the soon-to-be state of Kansas. The political storm turned into years of attack-and-revenge between gangs on horseback. "Bushwhackers"

1866

For the first time, cowboys drive cattle through Texas up to Abilene, KS, on the Chisholm Trail.

A first for American women: **Lucy Beaman Hobbs** becomes a licensed dentist.

Jan. 9 — Fisk School for black students is founded at Nashville, TN. As of 1867, it will be Fisk University.

Sept. 7 — Telegraph messages can be sent across the ocean thanks to **Cyrus W. Field**'s transatlantic cable.

and "jayhawkers" burned farms and towns, stole, killed, and kidnapped as they rampaged over the bleeding Missouri-Kansas border. Country folks like the Carvers were caught in the middle.

Kidnapped!

One night, raiders strung Moses up and burned his feet with hot coals, trying, without success, to get the old man to say where his money was buried. He was stubborn. When marauders

1867

Baseball pitcher **William Arthur "Candy" Cummings** of Brooklyn, NY, invents the curve ball.

Christopher Latham Sholes of Milwaukee, WI, invents the typewriter.

Alfred Nobel of Sweden invents dynamite.

Johann Strauss, Jr. composes "The Blue Danube."

Feb. 7 —
Laura Ingalls Wilder, author, is born in Wisconsin.

March 30 —
The Congress agrees to a deal made by Secretary of State **William H. Seward.** The U.S. will pay Russia $7,200,000 for Alaska territory, a.k.a. "Seward's Folly."

came again, they stole away Mary and two of her little ones. Moses Carver asked one of his friends to ride into Arkansas to search for them. As George would write, "only I was brought back, nearly dead with whooping cough with the report that mother and sister were dead, although some say they saw them afterwards going north with the soldiers."

Mary was lost to history. All George would have of his parents would be whatever others remembered: his mother's spinning wheel and the record of her purchase. As a reward for

Moses and Susan looked after Mary's sons.

1867

July 9 —
The 14th
Amendment
is ratified.
Former slaves
shall be
U.S. citizens.

1868

Nov. 7 —
**Marie Sklodowska
Curie,** *physicist, is
born in Poland
(see 1903).*

**Louisa May
Alcott** *writes*
Little Women.

Engineer **Robert
Whitehead**
*develops the first real
torpedo, and* **George
Westinghouse**
*invents air brakes
that will safely stop
speeding trains.*

the return of the child, Moses parted with one of the fine horses. Now he and Susan would look after Mary's sons, and they would have Carver for a last name. For six-year-old Jim and his coughing, gasping baby brother George, it was a harsh beginning.

THE LARGER WORLD

OF COURSE, LOADS OF LIFE WAS GOING ON in the world into which George was born. Clipper ships and steamships were crisscrossing the oceans. There were little kids and babies about in the world who had no idea of their significance in some far-off year. Automobile maker Henry Ford was a 2-year-old in 1865. As for future U.S. Presidents, Theodore Roosevelt was seven and Warren G. Harding was a brand-new baby. Annie Oakley, who'd amaze audiences with her sharpshooting, was a 5-year-old Ohio girl. Out in California, Samuel Clemens, a 29-year-old, down-

1868

Japan's capital moves from Kyoto to Edo, renamed Tokyo.

May 26 —
Republicans want **President Andrew Johnson** out of office but he survives his impeachment trial in the U.S. Senate.

Nov. 3 —
War hero of the Union Army **Ulysses S. Grant** is elected 18th U.S. President.

on-his-luck reporter, was working on a funny story that'd be published under his new pen name, Mark Twain.

On one side of the world, thousands of laborers brought from China were hard at work on the U.S. transcontinental railroad. On the other, workers were building the Suez Canal. It will allow ships to sail through the northeastern corner of Africa from the Mediterranean to the Red Sea.

In the months before George Carver was born, thousands of Americans, black and white, were bleeding their lives out into

American versus American; brother against brother

1869

Welch's Grape Juice and Campbell's Soup have their beginnings this year.

Ships sail between the Red and the Mediterranean Seas on the newly completed Suez Canal.

Yokohama, Japan — **Jonathan Scobie** *invents the jinrikisha (rickshaw).*

Feb. 23 — **W. E. B. Du Bois,** *historian, educator, is born in Massachusetts.*

the fields and rivers of Virginia in the final battles of the truly terrible Civil War. It had killed more than 600,000 soldiers. On April 9, 1865, Confederate General Robert E. Lee surrendered his Army of Northern Virginia to U.S. General Ulysses S. Grant,

Assassin in the dark

signaling the end of the major fighting. A mere six days later, shocking news was spreading fast from Washington D.C.: 56-year-old Abraham Lincoln had been shot and mortally wounded. For the very first time, a U.S. President had been killed by an assassin.

Ships carried the terrible news to Europe, where Queen Victoria, 46, was in the 28th year of her reign over the vast British Empire. Fierce, forceful Otto von Bismarck, 50, was uniting the German Empire. Not until next year, 1866, would people finally, after repeated attempts, be able to send telegraphed messages by way of a huge cable snaking along the floor of the Atlantic

1869

May 10 —
Promontory Summit, Utah —
America's transcontinental railroad is completed with a golden spike.

June 1 —
Thomas A. Edison
patents an "electrographic vote recorder," his first major invention.

Dec. 10 —
A first for American women: The females of Wyoming Territory are granted the right to vote.

Ocean from Newfoundland to Ireland. And that's not the only technological breakthrough in the works.

In the first part of the Civil War, Thaddeus Lowe's manned balloons had helped the Union Army see what the Confederate forces were up to. Now, in 1865, he developed an ice machine, ancestor of modern refrigerators. A year after *microbe* (germ) buster Louis Pasteur invented pasteurization, Dr. Joseph Lister, 38, of England, builds upon Pasteur's work and revolutionizes surgery with the use of germ-killing antiseptics. Now patients who survive their operations will be less likely to die of infection. (Meanwhile, Pasteur, 42, was busy treating sick silkworms and saving France's silk industry.)

Inspired by the interior of slim Erie Canal boats, George Pullman, 34, designed the first railroad sleeping cars. Inspired by the peas in his garden, Gregor Mendel, 43, an Austrian *botanist* (one who studies plant life), was developing the science of *genetics* (how characteristics are passed on from one generation to the next).

Back in 1831, brilliant experimenter Michael Faraday had learned, among other things, how to use a magnet to generate electric current and make it flow through a wire. His work was

---

1870

Dmitri Mendeléev *of Russia and* **Julius Meyer** *of Germany discover that the properties of a chemical element depend on its atomic weight.*

Feb. 3 — *The 15th Amendment becomes law, giving black male citizens the right to vote, a civil right denied to U.S. females until 1920.*

Feb. 25 — **Senator Hiram R. Revels** *of Mississippi becomes the first African American elected to Congress.*

built upon the discoveries of Benjamin Franklin, Humphry Davy, and other scientists. Their work made it possible for young mathematician James Clerk Maxwell to figure out the equations that explained the relationship between electricity and magnetism. He was able to describe how these forces *undulate* (move in waves) and to prove mathematically that light is electromagnetic. Maxwell's 1865 ideas would be at the foundation of work that will be done by physicists such as Albert Einstein, whose life wouldn't begin until 1879.

The best-known African Americans of the era were a sturdy trio of abolitionists: Harriet Tubman (around 45 years old); Frederick Douglass (nearly 50), and Sojourner Truth (pushing 70). This year, at last, on December 18, 1865, they'd see slavery in the United States abolished once and for all. Now newly freed slaves cherished a hope that they might be allowed to vote. Their desire to participate in the workings of the nation was shared by all of America's women. But *suffrage* (the right to vote) was denied to such citizens as battlefield nurse Clara Barton, 44; Elizabeth Cady Stanton, 50; Susan B. Anthony, 45; and Maria Mitchell, 47, astronomy professor at New York's newly opened Vassar Female College. Not until 1920 would U.S. females be able to vote.

1870

July 12 —
Brothers **John** and **Isaiah Hyatt** launch the age of modern plastics when they patent celluloid.

July 19 —
Napoleon III of France declares war on Prussia, beginning a hungry, deadly time for the French people.

1871

Rome becomes the capital of the Kingdom of Italy. Germany's crazy quilt of kingdoms and principalities unites under the rule of **Emperor Wilhelm I** and his "Iron Chancellor," **Count von Bismarck.**

March 3 —
No longer will America's native tribes be officially regarded as independent nations. By an Act of Congress, Indians shall be wards of the U.S. Government.

A GREEN THUMB AND A HUNGRY MIND

FREEDOM MEANT THAT MARY'S SONS went from being the Carvers' property to being their foster sons. The couple did their best to look after them. Still, it took a long time for puny little George to recover from his ordeal. In the years before a vaccination was developed in the 1930s, thousands of little ones died when their throat and lungs were racked with whooping cough. George survived, of course. While Jim, his sturdy big brother, worked out in the fields with "Uncle Mose," sickly George helped "Aunt Susan." Working alongside her, he learned how to cook, sew, and do the laundry. These were handy skills for anyone to have, but they'd be crucial for George Carver, as you'll see.

As George drew and embroidered, Aunt Susan saw his artistic talent. As he took to reading and pored over their old

---

1871   **1872**

April 10 —
Brooklyn, NY —
Phineas T. Barnum
opens the Great Traveling
Museum, Menagerie, Caravan,
and Hippodrome. Next year, his
Greatest Show on Earth will be
the first circus to travel by train.

Oct. 8 – 14 —
Chicago, IL —
Nearly 300 people
die and 90,000 are
made homeless by a
fire begun, some say,
by a cow kicking
over a lantern.

Thomas Adams
invents sticks of
chewing gum,
licorice-flavored
"Blackjack."

blue-bound copy of *Webster's Elementary Spelling Book*, she and Moses had to have noticed how smart George was. He peppered them with questions about everything from the weeds by the road to the pet rooster perched on his foster father's shoulder. Fiddle-playing Moses must have gotten a bang out of how much the skinny little boy liked music and singing.

George loved music.

1872

Horticulturist **Luther Burbank** *develops a new, improved potato.*

March 1 —
The U.S. Congress establishes Yellowstone National Park.

May 10 —
Victoria Claflin Woodhull *is the first woman to run for U.S. President.* **Frederick Douglass** *is her running mate on the Equal Rights Party ticket.*

George loved working in the garden. He wanted to know about everything that lived there, animal, vegetable, or mineral, from the tallest corn to the lowliest potato bug. Soon he was experimenting on his own, trying to find out what sort of soil suited each flower and vegetable. How might a sick plant be encouraged, a dying plant be saved? Young George seemed to know just what to do. It wasn't long before folks were going to that green-thumbed Carver kid and asking *him* questions! They called him the plant doctor.

1872

June 27 —
Paul Lawrence Dunbar, *African American poet, is born in Ohio.*

July 4 —
President **Calvin Coolidge** *is born in Vermont.*

Nov. 5 —
Suffrage activist **Susan B. Anthony** *is arrested for voting in the national election.*

1873

James Clerk Maxwell *publishes his* Treatise on Electricity and Magnetism.

Jules Verne *publishes* Around the World in 80 Days (see 1889).

1873

Aug. 1 —
Andrew S. Hallidie introduces his invention, the cable car, to the streets of San Francisco.

Oct. 27 —
So long to the open range, thanks to barbed wire, the invention that **Joseph Glidden** patented today.

Philadelphia, PA —
Richard Green invents the ice-cream soda.

25

As he grew, George took to rambling into the woods, coming home loaded down with rocks and all sorts of plants and creatures. His folks saw what a special, curious kid George was. Still, Aunt Susan didn't want his "specimens" cluttering up her cabin, especially if they were still crawling, flying, hopping, or slithering! She made him empty his pockets out in the yard.

As George would write, he "wanted to know every strange stone, flower, insect, bird, or beast." But there was no one to teach him. Looking back, he said it was as if "his very soul was thirsty for an education."

George makes a friend.

Because of their race, the Carver boys had been turned away from their neighborhood school. Some say that when a young educated fellow passed through their corner of Missouri, Moses and Susan hired him to give the boys some lessons, but precocious George had more questions than the tutor had answers. Then, when George was about 12, he heard of a

1874

Gold in the Black Hills! Ignoring dangers and U.S. promises not to trespass on Lakota Sioux reservation land, prospectors rush to Dakota Territory.

April 25 — **Guglielmo Marconi,** inventor of the radio, is born in Italy.

May 14 — Athletes from Harvard and Canada's McGill University meet in Boston, MA, and invent modern football.

July 4 — A mighty Mississippi River bridge, designed by **James B. Eads,** opens at St. Louis, MO.

George sets off on his quest.

class for black students over in the town of Neosho. The eight miles he walked to get there were the beginning of years of wandering, looking for what some kids took for granted: an education. George never again lived with the Carvers, although he visited them often. He was on a quest.

1874

Aug. 10 —
President **Herbert
Hoover** *is born
in Iowa.*

Nov. 7 —
Cartoonist
Thomas Nast
*comes up with
a symbol for the
Republican Party:
the elephant.*

1875

Mark Twain
publishes The
Adventures of
Tom Sawyer.

*Folks are riding
high-wheeler
bicycles a.k.a.
penny-farthings.*

A seeker on his own

CHAPTER TWO

Sunshine and Shadow

The Wandering Years

OR YOUNG GEORGE CARVER, the period between 1877 and 1890 was a restless time, full of loyal friends and hard, hard work. "Sunshine and shadow" was how he'd describe this time later on. He was a poor, brilliant black teenager — a "defenseless orphan," who had to earn his own way in the world. Discouraging, even terrifying incidents littered his path to becoming an educated man.

In Neosho, Missouri, George met Andrew and Mariah Watkins, a childless black couple who offered him a home in return for help with the chores. "Aunt Mariah" was wise in the

1875

Jan. 14 —
Albert Schweitzer, *musician, doctor, author, and winner of the Nobel Peace Prize for his medical missionary work in Africa, is born in Germany.*

May 17 —
*Louisville, KY —
Aristedes wins the first running of the Kentucky Derby.*

Aug. 24 —
Matthew Webb, *27, is the first person to swim across the English Channel: 21 miles from Dover to Calais in 21 hours, 45 minutes.*

A lesson from Aunt Mariah

ways of medicinal plants (knowledge she would share with her young boarder) and helping women bring their babies into the world. She needed a hand with the laundry, and that George knew how to do. He came to admire Mrs. Watkins. His new school teacher was another matter.

1876

Korea becomes an independent nation.

BELL

March 7 — **Alexander Graham Bell** *is issued patent no. 174,465 for his telephone (see 1915).*

June 25 — *Montana Territory —* In the Battle of Little Bighorn, **Crazy Horse** *and some 2,500 Lakota warriors kill 262 U.S. soldiers and* **George Armstrong Custer,** *the reckless Army officer who led his men into harm's way.*

George at school

Mr. Frost was confronted with an intense, skinny country boy with shabby clothes, an oddly high-pitched voice (a souvenir, perhaps, of his early illness), and more eager questions than the schoolmaster could handle. George made the best of his opportunity. He studied and dug deeply into what books were available. In between, he was either plugging away at the washtubs or going to the A.M.E. (African Methodist Episcopal) Church with Aunt Mariah. His character was very much shaped by that of his industrious, very religious landlady. Like her, George saw no sense in wasting time, so when he figured that

1876

July 4 — *Philadelphia, PA* — *A painting by* **Edward M. Bannister,** *African American artist, wins first prize at the Centennial Exposition.*

Nov. 7 —
In the presidential election, 247,448 fewer votes are cast for **Rutherford B. Hayes** *than for* **Samuel Tilden**. *After months of terrible wrangling, a dubious deal was made:* **Hayes,** *the Republican, would be President, and U.S. troops would quit patrolling the South, thus ending Reconstruction.*

he'd learned all he could in Neosho, the 13-year-old hitched a ride out of town.

Drawn by the lure of reinventing one's life in the West, some 25,000 freed black folks moved to Kansas in the 1870s.

Adventuring into the unknown

George was one of them. Some settled in Nicodemus, the first western town built by and for black settlers, in 1877 (see map, pages 70–71). In the past troubled decades, "Free Kansas" had been famous for its *abolitionist* (anti-slavery) population. This did not mean that all white Kansans welcomed poverty-stricken black folks into their schools or into competition with them for jobs. In Kansas, George would have experiences both good and bad. And he would learn for himself what sodbusters, black or white, soon discovered: The high prairie was long on beauty and short on water. Plowing through the tough grassland and putting in a crop was a backbreaking job for man and beast.

1877

Thomas A. Edison *invents the phonograph.*

Canals on Mars? No, but people wonder after Italian astronomer **Giovanni Shiaparelli** *detects lines on the planet's surface.*

Oct. 5 — **Chief Joseph** *of the Nez Percé surrenders to U.S. forces. He and his people struggled but failed to get to Canada, having been forced out of their Oregon homeland. They must go to Indian Territory in Oklahoma.*

For now, in 1878, George sent word to Moses and Susan Carver that he'd found work and a place to live in Fort Scott, Kansas. He wouldn't be there long, thanks to ugly forces at work in the land.

RECONSTRUCTION

AFTER THE CIVIL WAR, Americans set about trying to rebuild their wrecked country. Lawmakers struggled to reunite the nation in a period known as Reconstruction. Officially, it lasted from 1865 until 1877, when U.S. troops finally pulled out of the southern states that had once been the Confederacy. When the 14th Amendment to the Constitution was ratified in 1868, African Americans became U.S. citizens. In 1870, the 15th granted black men the right to vote. (Most U.S. women, whatever race they were, would have to keep waiting.) But it was going to

1878

Turkey's at war with Russia and with Greece.

Composers **William S. Gilbert** and **Arthur S. Sullivan** *publish their operetta* H.M.S. Pinafore.

Cincinnati, OH —
Chemists at the Procter & Gamble Company announce the invention of floating Ivory Soap.

Albert A. Michelson, *American physicist, publishes a paper: "On a Method of Measuring the Velocity of Light." He will measure the speed of light, the diameter of stars, and the motion of Earth.*

At the Freedmen's Bureau

take more than 12 years and a few government programs to undo the human damage done by total war and 200 years of slavery. Nowadays, we are *still* experiencing the aftereffects.

Reconstruction was a complex, painful era and those who were hurt the most were the newly freed slaves in the South. As is always true, freedom wasn't free. Some 40,000 black troops had lost their lives in the Civil War, mostly as Union soldiers, fighting for their freedom. Ending the troubles caused by slavery would be costly, too. The U.S. was faced with nearly four million freed folks, many of whom were broke, homeless, and suffering

1878   **1879**

The people of Deadwood, Dakota Territory, are deathly ill with smallpox. As she cares for them day and night, **Martha "Calamity Jane" Canary** becomes a hero.

Feb. 21 —
New Haven, CT—
The first telephone directory is published. It has 50 listings.

British troops in South Africa massacre thousands of Zulu tribesmen.

from a lack of schooling and medical care. In 1865, the Congress set up an agency known as the Freedmen's Bureau to help.

More than 4,300 schools were founded, and at first, idealistic white folks signed up to teach newly freed blacks. As time passed, however, enthusiasm faded. Budgets tightened. Some schools grew shabby, understaffed, fewer and farther between. Still, there were those that blossomed into outstanding black educational institutions, such as Fisk University, in Nashville, Tennessee; Howard University, in the nation's capital, and Virginia's Hampton Institute (now Hampton University). That's where ex-slave Booker T. Washington was both student and teacher. You'll read more about him later.

It would be desperately inconvenient to be an African American in the racist U.S.A. well into the 20th century. In the later 1800s, there were furious folks who simply would not accept that former slaves could be equal, full-fledged citizens, never mind what the Constitution said. Men determined to keep black folks down grouped together, most famously in the Ku Klux Klan (see time line, 1865). Masked, hooded, white-robed riders rampaged through the nights. They terrorized and killed blacks and anyone who took their side. In fact, in 1897,

1879

People by the thousands travel to Menlo Park, NJ, to see **Thomas A. Edison's** newest invention: the first practical incandescent electric light bulb.

1880

March 14 — **Albert Einstein**, physicist, is born in Germany.

Dec. 21 — Dictator **Joseph Stalin** is born in Asia, east of the Black Sea.

France colonizes the African Congo and annexes the island of Tahiti.

when George referred to the night his infant self, sister, and mom were kidnapped, he wrote, "[we] were ku klucked."

JIM CROW

RIGID CODES OF BEHAVIOR designed to keep the races as separate as possible in all public places were put in place. The penalties for breaking these "Jim Crow" laws could be humiliating, harsh, or even deadly. One day in 1884, for example, conductors forced a 22-year-old black teacher from her seat in the ladies' car of a Tennessee train. Later, as a journalist, Ida Bell Wells-Barnett never stopped working for justice for her people and an end to lynching, a particularly fiendish part of America's culture in the decades surrounding the turn of the 19th and 20th centuries. It went something like this: White men would catch some unlucky someone, generally an African American male who was

---

1880

The first photograph reproduced in a newspaper is printed in The New York Daily Graphic.

Nov. 2 —
James A. Garfield defeats **Winfield Hancock** in the presidential election (see 1881).

1881

Inventor **John McTammany** patents a player piano that produces music using rolls of perforated paper.

thought to have stepped out of line. Then they'd beat him up and hang him, often in the presence of a crowd of people. Over the decades, throughout America, thousands of people were killed in such *unpunished* attacks.

A lynching

In Fort Scott, Kansas, young George Carver had an unforgettable look at the trouble that could befall an outnumbered person. It happened on March 26, 1879. A black man was captured. Folks said he'd raped a young white girl. That night, masked men broke into the jail and dragged the fellow out past a crowd of townspeople. Among the onlookers was George, a skinny black kid who supported himself by taking in laundry. He was no stranger to violent injustice, but nothing prepared him for what he saw next. The fellow was dragged right past him, then the crowd "dashed [the accused man's] brains out onto the sidewalk. As young as I was," grownup George would remember, "the horror haunted me and does even now."

1881

Clara Barton *becomes the first president of the American Red Cross.*

March 13 — **Czar Alexander II** *of Russia is mortally wounded by an assassin's bomb.*

July 2 — Washington, DC — *An assassin shoots* **James A. Garfield,** *who dies on Sept. 19.* **Vice President Chester A. Arthur** *becomes the 21st President.*

Oct. 26 — Arizona Territory — Tombstone's marshal **Virgil Earp,** *his brother* **Wyatt, "Doc" Holliday,** *and others engage in a shootout at the O.K. Corral.*

Imagine how scared he must have been. George hit the road north out of town as quickly as he could.

In the village of Olathe, Kansas, he found a school and a new pair of stand-in parents, ex-slaves Ben and Lucy Seymour. As usual, George found folks with washing that needed doing. It involved a lot more than pushing buttons or turning knobs. Doing the laundry meant pumping and hauling water. Chopping wood for fire to heat the water. Sorting, boiling, scrubbing, and rinsing. George wrung water out of heavy, dripping sheets and coarse work pants and hung them out to dry.

Prairie dogs

Later, when the Seymours moved out West to little Minneapolis, Kansas, George did, too. Knowing him as we do, we can be sure that he noticed the bluestem and wild rye grasses, fluttering with butterflies, dotted with all manner of wildflowers, and punctuated with prairie dogs.

It was summertime, 1880. George's country was quickly becoming an industrial giant. Back East, millions of European immigrants were pouring into the U.S.

1882

Chinese folks in the U.S. have faced racism and attacks for years, mainly in the West. Now the Congress passes a law closing the door to Chinese immigrants. It won't be opened until 1943 when China and the U.S. are allies, battling Japan.

Jan. 30 —
President **Franklin Delano Roosevelt** is born in New York.

Aug. 20 —
Moscow, Russia —
Peter Tchaikovsky's 1812 Overture has its first performance.

Soon they'd be hard at work in factories and down in the mines alongside other Americans. Out West, cowboys were herding market-bound cattle up the trails past sections closed off with barbed wire, Joseph Glidden's 1873 invention. U.S. soldiers and warriors of the western tribes were fighting over possession of the plains and mountains.

At or near the heart of the Plains Indians' way of life was the bison. Its muscle and skin provided them food, clothing, and shelter. By the 1880s, millions of these beasts had been slaughtered by white hunters — or soon would be. Many a railroad traveler delighted in shooting "buffalo" from the windows of a speeding train.

Thunder on the prairie

1882

New York — *For the first time, a Christmas tree is decorated with electric lights.*

1883

Ex-Pony Express rider, scout, buffalo-hunter **William F. Cody** *opens his Wild West Circus, soon to be known worldwide as Buffalo Bill's Wild West Show.*

May 24 — After 14 years of dangerous effort, the Brooklyn Bridge, designed by **John Augustus Roebling,** *is open.*

Edison's brightest invention

Nearly 90,000 miles of railroad crisscrossed the continent. The Mississippi was lively with barges, but steamboats, with their churning wheels and soaring smokestacks, ruled the river. Folks who delighted in the latest technology were telephoning one another, thanks to inventor Alexander Graham Bell (see time line, 1876). In 1877, when George was doing laundry in Missouri, the greatest inventor of them all, Thomas Edison, was in New Jersey, devising his favorite invention: the phonograph. In 1879, when teenage George was in Kansas, studying by the light of a kerosene lamp, 32-year-old Edison, came up with the truly brilliant, revolutionary, incandescent light bulb.

1883

Aug. 14 —
Ernest E. Just,
*African-American
scientist, is born in
South Carolina.*

Aug. 24 —
*Indonesia —
More than 36,000 people
die in the explosive
eruption of the volcano*
Krakatoa.

1884

Baraboo, WI —
The **Ringling Brothers,**
*Albert, Otto, Alfred, Charles,
and John, begin their circus.
Two other brothers, August
and Henry, join later on.*

Minneapolis, Kansas, on the banks of the Solomon River, was George's home for about four years. He found a school there where he was able to take high school courses. He made friends among his white classmates and teachers. They, in turn, liked and admired smart, hardworking George. He could cook, paint, draw, do fancy needlework, and get music out of a *squeezebox* (accordion) or harmonica. At least one of his neighbors loaned him books, and the bank loaned him money for his laundry business. He set up his tubs in a shack in a place folks called Poverty Gulch.

George hangs the wash to dry.

1884

Paul Gottlieb Nipkow *of Germany invents a spinning, scanning device that will lead to modern television (see 1922).*

Bolivia becomes a landlocked nation when a war is settled between Chile and Peru, and new boundaries are established.

Mark Twain *publishes* The Adventures of Huckleberry Finn.

GEORGE'S America was full of inventive folks.

1. This painter/inventor developed the telegraph (1830s–40s).

2. Every rainy day millions of drivers use this woman's invention: windshield wipers, patented in 1903.

3. After inventing the telephone (1876), he applied his creativity to such interests as aviation and helping the deaf.

4. The greatest inventor of them all patented 1,093 methods or devices.

5. He totally popularized photography with his Brownie camera (1900).

6. This black American inventor patented more than 35 ways of improving communication and transportation.

7. He invented the first synthetic plastic (1909).

8. These brothers made history when they flew their engine-powered invention into the sky (1903).

9. In Paris, France, he flew his lighter-than-air craft around the Eiffel Tower (1901).

10. Karl Benz and Gottlieb Daimler invented the gasoline-powered "horseless carriage," but it was this man, with his well-designed, mass-produced cars, who put millions of folks behind the wheel.

11. This radio pioneer sent the first wireless message (1895).

12. "That's the real McCoy" is an old expression. It came from one of this African American's many inventions: a device that kept train engines oiled and running smoothly.

received a patent for her design of a fold-out bed (1885).

In a first for black women, Sarah E. Goode

For instance, Margaret E. Knight made a safety device for textile looms in 1850, the first of her many inventions, when she was only 12.

⑧ Wilbur and Orville Wright (1867~1912) (1871~1948)

① Samuel F.B. Morse (1791~1872)

⑨ Alberto Santos-Dumont (1873~1932)

⑪ Guglielmo Marconi (1874~1937)

⑦ Leo Baekeland (1863~1944)

⑥ Granville T. Woods (1856~1910)

⑫ Elijah McCoy (1843~1929)

⑤ George Eastman (1854~1932)

② Mary Anderson (1866~1953)

④ Thomas Alva Edison (1847~1931)

③ Alexander Graham Bell (1847~1922)

⑩ Henry Ford (1867~1947)

Early risers saw lanky George tramping through the country-side in the dim dawns. These morning walks would be a lifelong

Out in the countryside

habit of his. They allowed him to check out the local *flora and fauna* (plants and animals). They were a time of meditation, too, sort of like prayers. He never segregated his religion from his scientific interest in the natural world. For George Washington Carver, the two were totally integrated. Years later, this is one way he explained his point of view: "More and more as we come closer and closer in touch with nature and its teachings we are able to see the Divine."

It was during these years that George went back to Diamond to visit the Carvers. In 1883, he learned that smallpox had killed his brother, Jim. "Being conscious as never before that I was left alone," George remembered, "I trusted God and pushed ahead."

1884

May 8 —
President **Harry S. Truman** *is born in Missouri.*

Nov. 4 —
Grover Cleveland *is elected. He'll be the 22nd U.S. President.*

Louis Pasteur *develops a rabies vaccine.*

1885

Both **Gottlieb Daimler** and **Karl Benz** *come up with successful gasoline engines. Gottlieb uses his to build the first real motorcycle. Karl puts his in a wheeled carriage, a.k.a. the first automobile.*

Rejected!

George did push ahead. He added typing to his skills and got a job in Missouri as an office clerk in the Kansas City train station. As eager as ever for more education, George mailed an application to a Presbyterian college up in the northeast corner of Kansas. It's easy to imagine his thrill in opening the letter that said he'd been accepted. George's words help us imagine his next feelings: "When the President [of Highland College] saw I was colored he would not receive me."

1885

Englishman **J. K. Starley** *manufactures the first commercially successful "safety" bike, a bicycle with same-size wheels.*

Amazing sharpshooter **Annie Oakley** *joins Buffalo Bill's Wild West Show.*

July 1 — **King Leopold II** *of Belgium establishes a colony in the Congo (now the Democratic Republic of the Congo) so he could plunder its rubber, copper, and other resources. Many Africans died under the Belgians' cruel treatment.*

George had spent nearly all of his money, and his confidence was crushed. It'd be years before he'd even try to go to college again. Now it was back to the washtubs or whatever work he could find.

HOME ON THE PRAIRIE

A YEAR LATER FOUND HIM IN AN ENTIRELY DIFFERENT SETTING: Far and away in windy, western Kansas, George Washington Carver was a homesteader. He bought a *quarter section* (half a mile square or 160 acres) in late summer, 1886. With borrowed equipment he planted corn, a garden, and trees. He dug wells, but never found much water. When George wasn't sweating over his crops, vegetables, and washtubs or caring for his chickens, he made music for his friends thereabouts and went to church on Sundays. What's more, by April 1887, he'd cut, lifted, and stacked

1886

Atlanta, GA —
Pharmacist **John S. Pemberton** *begins selling the new headache remedy he's invented: Coca-Cola.*

Waco, TX —
Chemist **R. S. Lazenby** *introduces his new soft drink: Dr Pepper.*

May 4 —
Labor movement turns deadly. Chicago's Haymarket Square is crowded with folks striking for an 8-hour workday when someone throws a bomb, killing 8 policemen. Many are killed when police charge into the mob, guns blazing (see Nov. 11, 1887).

heavy blocks of earth until he'd completed a little sod house on the prairie. It was 14 feet square and rather dark inside. Bugs felt right at home in the earthen walls, but at least the walls were thick, making the indoors cool in summer, warm in winter.

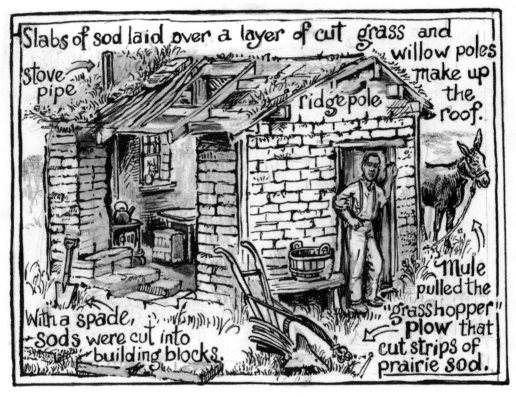

Little "soddy" on the western prairie

1886

June 3 —
Grover Cleveland, *the only President to get married in the White House, is wed to* **Frances Folsom.**

Sept. 4 —
After years of fighting on the Mexican border, U.S. troops capture Apache warrior **Geronimo.**

Oct. 28 —
New York Harbor —America's gift from the French people, **Frédéric Auguste Bartholdi's** *sculpture of the Statue of Liberty, is dedicated by* **President Cleveland.**

The winter of 1887–88, however, had a big surprise in store for Westerners. Just as the ocean recedes from the beach before the tsunami rushes in, the icy weather turned balmy on January 12, 1888, just before a truly epic blizzard blasted across the Great Plains, killing as many as 500 people and thousands of cattle. You can get an idea of what it must have been like in *The Long Winter*. In that book, Laura Ingalls Wilder tells how she and her hungry family, up in Dakota Territory, suffered through the bitter cold and darkness.

1887

Arthur Conan Doyle *publishes* A Study in Scarlet, *his first story about detective* **Sherlock Holmes.**

Florida lawmakers pass a Jim Crow law: Black and white railroad passengers must be kept apart from each other.

COLORED SEATING ONLY

Heinrich Hertz *of Germany is studying and identifying electromagnetic waves.*

A *bitter, blasting blizzard*

George Carver was about 23 years old when he weathered the blizzard of '88. Whether it was the killer storm or a young man's restlessness, he decided to put the frontier behind him. As the 1880s came to an end, so did the Kansas chapter of his life. The next would be in Iowa. There, at last, George would fulfill his quest for knowledge. Doors he'd never imagined would be opened to him.

1887

Nov. 11 —
With no proof of guilt, four anarchists are hanged for the May 1886 deaths in Haymarket Square.

1888

Nikola Tesla *invents an electric motor and inventor* **George Eastman** *introduces his Kodak box camera.*

London, England —
Six women are killed by the mysterious **Jack the Ripper.**

Knowledge quest

CHAPTER THREE

THE GOLDEN DOOR OF FREEDOM

A REAL HUMAN BEING

ONE SUNDAY MORNING IN WINTERSET, IOWA, in a church whose members tended to be white, one of the ladies in the choir was charmed by the sound of a fine tenor voice coming from a young black man in the back of the congregation. On Monday morning, the lady and her husband, both prominent citizens in the town, invited the singer to dinner. Of course, it turned out that the fine singer was George, working those days as a cook in a local hotel.

Helen and John Milholland saw a slender young man with an earnest, handsome face, trimmed with a mustache. His long-

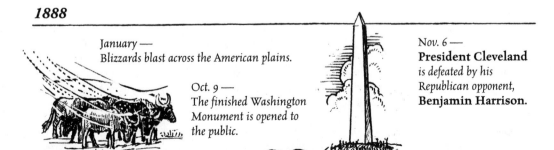

1888

January —
Blizzards blast across the American plains.

Oct. 9 —
The finished Washington Monument is opened to the public.

Nov. 6 —
President Cleveland is defeated by his Republican opponent, **Benjamin Harrison.**

fingered hands were rough from years of doing laundry, and a flower bloomed in the threadbare lapel of his shabby jacket. The couple quickly discovered that there was more to George Washington Carver than a sweet voice. Like Moses and Susan Carver, Aunt Mariah Watkins, and others who'd influenced him along the way, the Milhollands were impressed with his deep spiritual nature, his intelligence, and his many talents. In time, they encouraged him to try again to get into college.

That's just what he did.

If you happened to go back in time to the time-space inter-section of September 9, 1890, at Indianola, Iowa, you might see George. He wasn't the first, but right then he was the only black student at Simpson College. With his tubs, boiler, and wash-board, he'd still have to scrape out a living. He'd be broke most of the time, but at last he was getting what he most wanted: educa-tion and acceptance. As George would write, his fellow students "made me believe I was a real human being."

George studied English composition and grammar, arithmetic, singing, and piano, but he excelled in drawing. He was particularly good at painting flowers. After all, he still loved growing things. In his precious spare time, he'd experiment, with

1889

British soldiers begin using the first, fully automatic machine gun, developed by **Hiram Maxim,** American-born inventor.

Pittsburgh, PA — Steelworkers begin making I beams, the basis for skyscrapers' steel skeletons.

Chicago, IL — **Jane Addams** and **Ellen Starr** found Hull House to help immigrants get settled in America.

Emperor Menelik II unifies Ethiopia, establishing its capital in Addis Ababa.

April 20 — **Adolf Hitler,** dictator, is born in Austria.

plants, creating hybrids, for instance, by *cross-fertilizing* (combining cells) from two different kinds of vegetables, flowers, or fruit trees to create a new variety. Or he'd *graft* (attach) a *scion* (a bud or a cutting) from one plant to another so they'd grow together. Grafting is a way to *propagate* (reproduce) seedless plants or to improve the quality of an existing plant.

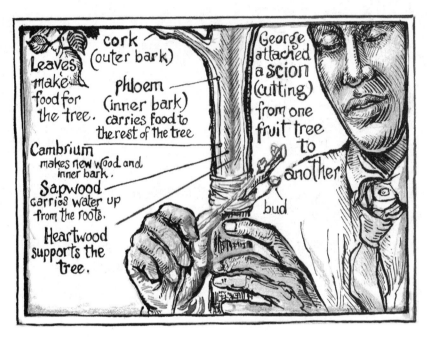

cork (outer bark)

Leaves make food for the tree.

phloem (inner bark) carries food to the rest of the tree

Cambrium makes new wood and inner bark.

Sapwood carries water up from the roots.

Heartwood supports the tree.

George attached a scion (cutting) from one fruit tree to another.

bud

Grafting

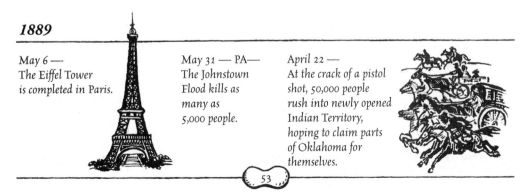

1889

May 6 —
The Eiffel Tower is completed in Paris.

May 31 — PA—
The Johnstown Flood kills as many as 5,000 people.

April 22 —
At the crack of a pistol shot, 50,000 people rush into newly opened Indian Territory, hoping to claim parts of Oklahoma for themselves.

Art class

His art professor respected George's talent, but still, she knew what a harsh place the United States was in the 1890s for African Americans. Miss Budd and her poverty-stricken student had to wonder if even a very gifted black artist could possibly make a living as a painter. What if, as Miss Budd suggested, George followed his interest in plants? What if he went to the state agricultural college (now known as Iowa State University) and studied something practical?

What if?

NELLIE BLY

1889

Nov. 14 —
Investigative reporter **Nellie Bly** *(a.k.a. Elizabeth Cochrane) sets out to outdo the hero of* **Jules Verne**'s *1873 novel* Around the World in 80 Days. *By ship, train, and stagecoach, Nellie circles the globe in 72 days, 6 hours, and 11 minutes, returning on Jan. 25, 1890.*

Nov. 20 —
Edwin P. Hubble, *astronomer, is born in Missouri.*

1890

Jacob Riis *becomes America's first photojournalist with his shocking book,* How the Other Half Lives, *about New York City's slums.*

THE GREATEST GOOD

❧

DEEPLY RELIGIOUS GEORGE WAS COMING TO BELIEVE that he must direct his talents to a higher purpose. In one of his many letters to Mrs. Milholland, he wrote, "God has a great work for me to do." What if he studied *agriculture* (the art and science of building fertile soil, raising healthy crops and animals)? Then he could use his education to help rural folks. He knew that ex-slaves were wearing themselves out down South trying to earn a living on land worn out from one cotton crop after another after another.

"The more my ideas develop, the more beautiful and grand seems the plan I have laid out to pursue, or rather," the young scientist wrote, "the one God has destined for me." For the huge challenge George was attempting, such confidence was definitely required.

1890

July 29 —
Vincent van Gogh, *painter, dies in France.*

Oct. 14 —
*President **Dwight D. Eisenhower** is born in Texas (see 1943).*

Nov. 17 – Dec. 29 —
*The native peoples in South Dakota are swept up in the Ghost Dance, a spiritual ritual. When U.S. officials mistake religion for rebellion, 12 Lakota Sioux die, including medicine man, **Sitting Bull.** Worse trouble flares at Wounded Knee Creek where 60 soldiers and 200 Lakota Sioux men, women, and children are massacred.*

SITTING BULL

In the summer of 1891, less than a year after he started at Simpson College, in Indianola, he left the many friends he'd made there. Now he would become the first and only black student at Iowa State College of Agriculture and Mechanical Arts, in the town of Ames, about 30 miles north of the state capital at Des Moines.

At first, he had to endure some name-calling and being ordered to eat his dormitory meals in the basement with the servants, but George set his mind to doing as he'd always done. He studied, went to church, and struggled to survive on what he could earn, steadfastly refusing to take money from anyone. Still, when it came to sketching and taking notes in class, George was grateful for his friends' pencil stubs and old wrapping paper.

Out on his morning walks, wearing his homemade clothes, thoughtful George tucked away specimens for his *herbarium* (plant collection). Not having money to head off to the market for groceries, George kept an eye out for berries and other, less obvious, foods in the wild. His time spent in the company of herb-wise Aunt Mariah Watkins had taught him plenty about dandelion greens, wild onions, and knowing which mushrooms were good eats and which had best be left alone.

1891

Springfield, MA — P. E. teacher **James A. Naismith** *invents basketball.*

The Kennedy Biscuit Works begins selling Fig Newton Cookies.

Thousands rush to find gold in Colorado Cripple Creek.

Brothers **Charles** *and* **Frank Duryea** *of Massachusetts test-drive their invention: America's first gasoline-powered automobile.*

George in his element

In the five years green-thumb George spent at Ames, he excelled in *botany* (the science of plants) and *horticulture* (the science and art of growing fruits, flowers, vegetables, and ornamental plants). George's most influential professor, Dr. Louis H. Pammel,

1892

New York —
Immigrants who've crossed the Atlantic Ocean will now come into America by way of Ellis Island.

Peter Tchaikovsky *composes* The Nutcracker *ballet.*

May 28 —
John Muir *starts the Sierra Club, America's first group organized to protect its environment.*

was a mycologist, one who studies fungi, such as mushrooms, mildews, molds, and lichens. They feed off plants, animals or rotting matter. Unlike other plants, a fungus has no *chlorophyll* (the substance that enables green plants to take energy from sunlight). Fungi do better in the dark. Some are harmful, causing Dutch elm disease or athlete's foot. Others, such as the sort of yeast that makes bread rise or molds that rot old trees and turn them into soil, are useful. Either way, George was fascinated. Each and every plant was doing exactly what God intended.

"Each created thing," he'd write, expressing a key part of his beliefs, "is an indispensable factor of the great whole." Before he left college, he became an expert researcher and collector of more than a thousand (!) fungus specimens.

Fungi

1892

June 29 — Homestead, PA — When workers strike for decent wages, **Andrew Carnegie**'s steel company hires 300 burly strike breakers. Four deaths and hundreds of injuries later, men go back to work for the same old pay.

Nov. 8 —
Grover Cleveland is elected to his second nonconsecutive term as President.

1893

Wealthy planters force Hawaiian **Queen Liliuokalani** from her throne, a first step to the islands' becoming a U.S. territory (see 1900).

COLLEGE MAN

GEORGE MADE GOOD GRADES AND LOYAL FRIENDS. Besides being a good guy at heart, he was certainly smart enough to know that being nice was a necessary survival skill. His genuine warmth and enthusiasm on top of all his many abilities helped most people to get past whatever mean, ignorant notions they might have had about George being a Negro, or "colored," as African Americans were commonly known back then.

He was active in all sorts of church and YMCA (Young Men's Christian Association) activities as well as clubs on campus. He drilled with the college's military unit. When the football players needed a trainer, he rubbed the athletes' aching muscles. When music was called for or students were asked to recite a funny or dramatic poem, or a play was being cast, there was George, ready to perform, which he did, often.

1893   *1894*

Whitcomb L. Judson *patents what will be known as the zipper.*

May 5 —
A price drop on Wall Street starts a few years of terrible economic times in the U.S.

March 25 —
Jacob S. Coxey *leads hundreds of ragged, unemployed folks, "Coxey's Army," on a march from Massillon, Ohio, to Washington, DC. Will the President or any Congressmen see them when they get there? Nope.*

George might have abandoned the idea of being a full-time artist, but he'd never given up painting. Imagine his excitement when he heard, in 1892, that Iowa's artists were invited to enter their work in a show. Imagine his gloom when he realized that

it meant getting himself and his paintings clear over to Cedar Rapids, a hundred miles away. He couldn't afford a trip like that. Nice idea, but impossible. Forget it. End of story — or was it?

No. George's friends bundled him into a buggy and took him to town, where they bought him a new suit and a train ticket. As if all of this kindness were not glory enough, four of his paintings at the state exhibit were chosen to represent Iowa at one of the greatest world's fairs ever: the 1893 World's Columbian Exposition in Chicago, Illinois.

A new suit of clothes

1894

May 11 – Aug. 6 — Chicago, IL — **George Pullman**'s employees take a 25 percent pay cut but still must live in pricey houses owned by Pullman. They strike (stop work). Other railroaders refuse to connect Pullman cars, jamming train traffic all over the Midwest, so **President Cleveland** sends soldiers. The strike ends in deadly violence.

Nov. 1 — **Czar Alexander III** dies. His 24-year-old son **Nicholas** becomes Russia's absolute ruler (see 1918).

THE WORLD'S COLUMBIAN EXPOSITION, 1893

People went to fairs in London (1851), Paris (1867), Philadelphia (1876), and more to experience the latest that the world's manufacturers, governments, and peoples had to offer.

The Chicago fair in 1892 was meant to mark 400 years since Columbus came to the Americas, but difficulties delayed it until 1893. It attracted more than 26 million visitors. At first, Ida Bell Wells-Barnett urged other blacks to stay away because they hadn't been invited to showcase their achievements. In the end, Frederick Douglass, the old orator, and author Paul Lawrence Dunbar were among the African Americans who were allowed to present their ideas on August 25, 1893—Colored People's Day.

John Philip Sousa's famous band was just one part of the Chicago World's Fair along with Buffalo Bill's Wild West Show and replicas of Columbus's three ships, sent all the way from Spain. Soaring above it all was the giant, turning Ferris wheel, 250 feet in diameter.

1895

John Harvey Kellogg *introduces dry breakfast cereal to the world, and* **King C. Gillette** *invents the safety razor.*

New York City newspaper The World *prints the first popular comic strip,* "Hogan's Alley," *drawn by* **Richard F. Outcault.**

German physicist **Wilhelm K. Röntgen** *discovers X-rays.*

Until George received his Bachelor of Science degree in 1894, no black student had ever graduated from Iowa State. Over the next two years, he worked toward his master's degree, studied fungi, and worked on scientific papers. He conducted horticultural experiments in the college's greenhouse, of which he was now in charge. Like many a graduate student then and now, he taught undergrads. Those who signed up for freshman biology may never before have had a black instructor — another first for Iowa State. They soon discovered that Assistant Botany Professor Carver had a natural gift for teaching.

George could, if he wished, keep on teaching in Iowa after he finished his graduate work. Or, he could agree to teach at a black agricultural college in Mississippi. Instead, in the spring of 1896, George accepted an offer from Booker T. Washington (BTW), the best-known black man in America, now that Frederick Douglass had passed away (in 1895).

Mr. Washington headed the vocational school he founded in Alabama and that he named after the town of Tuskegee. He was looking to hire a new teacher, and he very much wanted the brilliant young scientist he'd heard of who had an advanced degree in agriculture earned at a white northern college.

1895	1896		
March 22 — Paris, France — Brothers **Louis** and **Auguste Lumiere** use their new invention, the cinematograph, to show motion pictures to theatergoers (see 1907).	In Athens, Greece, male athletes compete at the first modern Olympic Games. Women will be allowed to take part in 1900.	Yukon Territory, Canada — Gold is discovered on the Klondike River. Thousands of hopefuls will rush to the far Northwest.	**John Philip Sousa,** leader of the greatest-ever marching band, writes "Stars and Stripes Forever."

Good-bye, so long!

George, for his part, very much admired the principal of Tuskegee and wholeheartedly agreed with the controversial ideas he'd expressed in Atlanta. According to the letter that George wrote to his new boss (he hoped), coming to Tuskegee would fulfill "the one ideal of my life to be of the greatest good to the greatest number of 'my people' possible and to this end I have been preparing myself for these many years."

So it was that George climbed aboard one southbound train after another until he got to Tuskegee, Alabama, in the autumn of 1896. It would be his home for the next 47 years.

1896

Henry Ford *builds a quadricycle, his first automobile.*

May 6 —
Washington, DC —
Smithsonian scientist
Samuel P. Langley
flies his steam-powered model airplane 3,000 feet along the Potomac River.

May 18 —
The Supreme Court rules on the case of Plessy v. Ferguson: Segregating black and white citizens is legal.

"In all things purely, social we can be as separate

BOOKER TALIAFERRO WASHINGTON (1856-1915)

TUSKEGEE AND BOOKER T.

Booker T. Washington was the son of an enslaved woman and the white man who owned both mother and son. Young Booker was nine years old when he heard that the Civil War was over. Now he and millions of other ex-slaves had their freedom and very little else. He struggled out of bitter poverty by digging coal and mining salt. Determined to earn an education, BTW became a student and, later on, an instructor at Hampton Institute at Hampton, Virginia. The goal of this and other such schools was teaching useful trades to newly freed slaves, equipping them to go out into the world, and teach others to free themselves with hard work and education. That became the mission of Booker T. Washington and the school he was determined to start.

On July 4, 1881, BTW and 30 students began the Tuskegee Normal and Industrial Institute in a leaky wreck of a church in rural Alabama. As the institute's founder and principal, BTW worked hard to build and expand his school. That meant writing books, newspaper articles, giving speeches, and coaxing money out of people's pockets so he could hire instructors for more students who needed, above all, job training. BTW thought that learning a trade was more important than studying the arts, literature, and history. To his way of thinking, civil rights and equal treatment would be a reward to African Americans who'd earned some money and property. He believed that as more and more black people taught, farmed, and worked in the building trades and in their local shops, restaurants, schools, and factories, their white neighbors would begin treating them with some respect.

dignity in tilling a field as in writing a poem." (1901)

as the five fingers, and yet as one as the hand in all things essential to mutual progress." (1875) "No race can prosper till it learns that there is as much

In many black households, BTW became known as a compromiser — even a traitor to his people — after a speech he gave in Atlanta, Georgia, in 1895. He said that blacks should quit demanding social and political equality. Instead, they should do their best to get along in a white world and work their way up from "the bottom of life." White America rewarded BTW with fame and access to Presidents. He advised both Theodore Roosevelt and William Howard Taft on racial policies and educational issues. Even before his untimely death in 1915 at age 59, his beliefs began to fall out of favor. These days, most public attitudes reflect those of W. E. B. Du Bois, his greatest critic (see page 90).

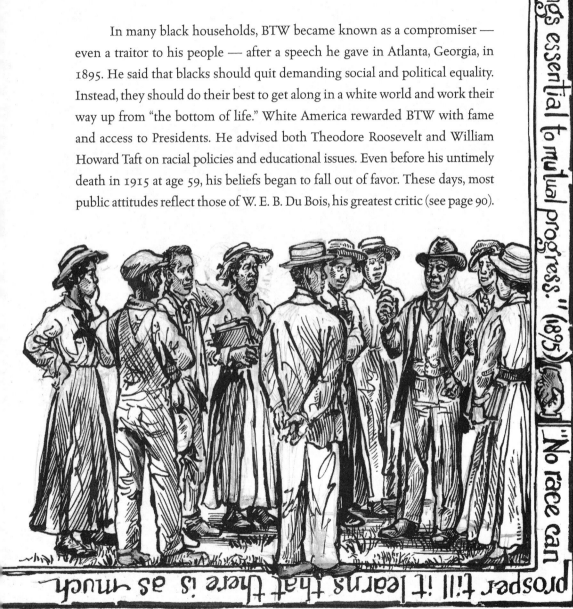

BOOKER T. WASHINGTON

GEORGE WASHINGTON CARVER

On the Institute's campus, in 1899, Tuskegee's faculty and students designed and built the OAKS, a fine brick house for BOOKER T. WASHINGTON, the founder

CHAPTER FOUR

BTW AND
GWC

RIDING THE SOUTHBOUND TRAIN

IT HAD TAKEN YEARS OF SLOGGING for George to become what he was, a popular teacher with close friends and serious, scientific work to do in a well-equipped laboratory. What's more, as a black man in nearly all-white Ames and in his academic community, George was special. In going to Alabama, he was giving up a lot. What was he getting?

For one thing, George, a 31-year-old bachelor, would earn an annual salary of $1,000. At the end of the 19th century, the average working man supported a family on about half that amount. For another, George savored the challenge of doing the

1896	1897
Nov. 3 — **William McKinley** *defeats* **William Jennings Bryan** *and will be the 25th U.S. President.*	**Bram Stoker,** *author, introduces the world to Dracula.*

Americans are introduced to Jell-O dessert, Grape Nuts breakfast cereal, and in Boston, their first subway. On April 19, they run a long way on purpose in the first Boston Marathon.

difficult for noble reasons. He truly felt that his talents were God-given and that he was God-chosen to teach his people how to restore their ruined land and their beaten-down selves. He felt sort of like a missionary: excited and humble. Truly special.

It's probably just as well that he couldn't look down the tracks into his immediate future.

On his way to Alabama

George Washington Carver had a lot to ponder in 1896, there on the trains carrying him and his trunks full of plant

1897

Twins **Francis** and **Freelan Stanley** *begin making their steam-powered Stanley Steamers.*

July 24 — **Amelia Earhart,** *aviator, is born in Kansas (see 1937).*

1898

Valdemar Poulsen *of Denmark invents a telegraphone, the first machine that records sound magnetically.*

Telegraphone

H. G. Wells, *author of* The Time Machine *(1895) and The Invisible Man (1897), writes* War of the Worlds *(see 1938).*

specimens farther and deeper into the South. As an African American born in slavery, it's likely that he was wary of going back into the heart of the former Confederacy. Certainly he was curious about what he would find there.

"When my train left the golden wheat fields and the tall green corn of Iowa for the acres of cotton, nothing but cotton, my heart sank a little," George would tell a radio audience in 1941. "The scraggly cotton grew close to the cabin doors, a few lonesome collards [greens], the only sign of vegetables; stunted cattle, bony mules; fields and hill sides cracked and scarred with gullies and deep ruts."

A little more than a century had passed since 1793, when Eli Whitney built his nifty little contraption that made cotton growing profitable. Whitney's cotton gin plus boatloads of slave labor led to a one-crop countryside. Folks raised cotton, from prosperous planters to *dirt farmers* (those who worked their own bit of land) and *sharecroppers* (those who worked their landlord's farm for a share of the crop). The plants sucked nutrients out of the earth. Years of burning off picked-over cotton stalks instead of plowing them back into the fields had turned soil into tired dirt, ready to wash away with the first hard rain.

1898	1899	
Feb. 15 – Aug. 12 — *An American ship USS Maine blows up—by accident, it turned out—off the coast of Spanish-controlled Cuba. This leads to war with Spain, U.S. takeover of the Philippine Islands, and an unlikely war hero:* **Theodore Roosevelt** (*see 1901*).	*Ragtime rocks America thanks to black pianist* **Scott Joplin**, *composer of the "Maple Leaf Rag." And "Lift Every Voice and Sing," a.k.a. black Americans' national anthem, is composed by brothers* **J. Rosamond** *and* **James W. Johnson** (*see 1920*).	 SCOTT JOPLIN

Forty-five years later, old George would still remember his first impression of the sunny South. There was "not much evidence of scientific farming anywhere." As far as he could see, "everything looked hungry; the land, the cotton, the cattle, and the people."

The stark scenes moving past his train window contrasted sharply with the picture that would play in the theater of the young scientist's mind. He could envision what at least a part of this land could be, with God's help and his own hard work. Tuskegee could become a green oasis in a mean desert of ruts and show the world what enlightened black people could do.

Earthly paradise

1899

American **Isadora Duncan** *revolutionizes the art of dance with her flowing costume and movement.*	*German scientist* **Herman Dreser** *discovers a swell remedy for headaches: acetylsalicylic acid, a.k.a aspirin.*	*Jan. 23 — A truly nasty guerrilla war breaks out between Filipinos and U.S. forces occupying the Philippine Islands (see 1901).*	*Oct. 12 — South Africa — Three years of Boer War begins as Dutch and British settlers begin fighting.*

As for any of the railroad conductors on any Southern train back then, none of George Washington Carver's abilities, lofty ideals, hard-earned college degrees, or the fact that he was making a big career move would have mattered. Back then, part of a conductor's job was to make sure that George or any other dark-skinned individual was seated in the "Colored Section." This sort of Jim Crow treatment had been customary for years. As of 1896, it was the official law of the land.

Whites up front; blacks to the back

When the Supreme Court justices ruled on a Louisiana case, *Plessy v. Ferguson*, they judged that it was perfectly constitutional for there to be "separate but equal" areas for black and white railroad passengers. For more than 50 years, the ruling would back up the *segregation* (separation) of practically every part of public life in the South, from buses to drinking fountains.

"Separate." Americans excelled at that. Any black child sweltering in sight of a public pool where he or she could not swim or studying a ratty old textbook in any of America's

---

1900

The *U.S. population is 76,212,168. The world population is up to 1.65 billion.*

L. Frank Baum *writes* The Wonderful Wizard of Oz.

Thousands of amateur photographers will be taking millions of pictures with their new $1 Brownie cameras made by **George Eastman***'s company.*

crumbling black schools knew that his or her countrymen had failed at "equal." The next century would be halfway over before this failure at fairness would even begin to be fixed. That was in 1954, long after George Washington Carver was dead and gone. That's when another case, *Brown v. Board of Education of Topeka* (Kansas) came before the nation's highest court. A new set of judges ruled that such segregation took away black citizens' constitutional rights to equal protection.

TURN OF THE CENTURY

AS THE SUN WAS SETTING ON THE 19TH CENTURY and rising on the 20th, Tuskegee's principal, Booker T. Washington, and his staff were getting used to the new man, and he was getting used to the Tuskegeans. As to what was going on in the mind of George Washington Carver — more about that later. What was going on in his world?

1900

Escape artist Ehrich Weiss, better known as **Harry Houdini,** begins his remarkable career this year.

Max Planck, *quantum physics pioneer, proposes the revolutionary idea that shining light is made of the smallest possible bits of energy: quanta.*

English archaeologist **Arthur Evans** *begins excavating the ancient palace at Knossos on the island of Crete.*

In 1900, the world had 1.6 billion human beings (compared with 6.6 billion of us now). Some of Earth's inhabitants were in deep trouble. Europeans, Americans, and Chinese living in northern China were killing one another (see time line, below). Filipinos in the Philippine Islands as well as native warriors in America's Southwest were fighting off U.S. soldiers. Superpower Great Britain was at war with South Africa's *Boers* (Dutch settlers). The beginning of the awesome, deadly 20th century was both remarkable and turbulent.

Guglielmo Marconi, 26, was tantalizingly close to being able to send a radio message across the Atlantic Ocean. In 1900, engineer Nikola Tesla, 44, could already imagine worldwide wireless communication by "television and telephone." He wrote, "We shall see and hear one another as perfectly as though we were face to face." *Physicist* (one who studies the fundamentals: time, matter, and energy) Max Planck, 42, offered this scientific groundbreaker: Radiating light was made out of *quanta* (particles of energy, smaller than atoms). Planck's quantum theory of energy inspired vivid thought experiments in the mind of Albert Einstein, a 21-year-old college graduate in Switzerland (see time line, 1905).

1900

In China, secret societies of peasants attack and kill Westerners and Chinese Christians. U.S. troops join rescuers from other nations to crush this "Boxer Rebellion."

Giacomo Puccini *composes his opera* Tosca.

June 14 —
Hawai'i becomes an official U.S. territory.

Sept. 8 —
As many as 10,000 people die when a huge hurricane pounds Galveston, Texas.

Wilbur and Orville

In Germany, Count Ferdinand von Zeppelin, 62, took his 420-foot-long, lighter-than-air ship for a test flight in 1900. Meanwhile, two Ohio fellows were out at the edge of North Carolina testing their passenger-carrying glider. Wilbur Wright, 33, wasn't too optimistic about their prospects. "Man will not fly for fifty years," he told his 29-year-old brother, Orville (see time line, 1903).

Babies — musician Louis Armstrong, for instance — were coming into the 20th-century world while elders such as Great Britain's 81-year-old queen, Victoria, were slipping away (see time line, 1901). On the Greek island of Crete, archaeologist Arthur Evans, 40, found the ruins of the palace of Knossos, built around 4000 B.C.E. On the island of Cuba, Theodore Roosevelt (TR) became an American hero in 1898, when he helped the U.S. defeat the tired, old Spanish Empire. When U.S. President

1901

Japanese-American chemist **Satori Kato** invents instant coffee.

In the Philippines, U.S. troops capture resistance fighter **Emilio Aguinaldo** and set up a government headed by **William Howard Taft** (see 1908).

Jan. 10 —
An awful lot of oil is discovered at Spindletop, near Beaumont, Texas. Oil drilling begins in Persia, a.k.a. Iran, but prospectors won't hit it big until 1908.

Jan. 22 —
Queen Victoria, 81, dies. Her son becomes **King Edward VII.** His empire includes the newly organized Commonwealth of Australia.

William McKinley, 57, was reelected later that year, TR became his Vice President. When an assassin's bullet killed McKinley in 1901, 42-year-old TR became the youngest man to take on the presidency. He'd be the most popular President, too, particularly among blacks when they heard that TR had invited Booker T. Washington to dinner on October 16, 1901. The men talked about the nation's "race problem" and, no doubt, *Up From Slavery,*

TR *and* BTW

BTW's autobiography, a 1901 bestseller. African Americans had been servants in the White House for a hundred years. The news that a black man was the President's guest was greeted with a blast of white-hot fury from loads of bull-headed, bigoted, mostly — but not entirely — Americans from the South.

1901

Sept. 6 —
Buffalo, NY —
William McKinley
is shot. When he dies on
September 14, **Vice**
President Theodore
Roosevelt *becomes the*
26th President.

Dec. 5 —
Walt Disney,
cartoonist, is born
in Chicago, IL.

Dec. 12 —
Guglielmo Marconi
and his coworkers send
the first-ever wireless
signal across the Atlantic,
from England to Canada.

Observation by observation, generation by generation,

FARADAY, botanist ASA GRAY, and biologist WILLIAM HARVEY.
(1810~1888) (1578~1657)

SCIENTISTS IN THE WORLD OF GEORGE WASHINGTON CARVER

1. His theory that plants and animals evolved over eons from a few shared ancestors caused people to rethink the nature of life on Earth, including their own.

2. This "census-taker of the sky" recorded and classified stars.

3. He proved that the heavens were an expanding universe of galaxies.

4. This black American chemist devised sight-saving and pain-relieving medicines.

5. He proved how diseases and germs were linked, then developed ways to fight them.

6. He made the life-saving discovery of germ-killing penicillin.

7. He found out how genes are arranged in our cells' chromosomes.

8. He pioneered *genetics* (the science of heredity).

9. Time, space, gravity, matter, and energy — the 20th century's best-known scientist revolutionized people's thinking about these concepts.

10. This team of physicists researched uranium's natural radioactivity.

11. Her books alerted people to the ways pollution and pesticides were hurting our planet.

12. This black American biologist advanced our knowledge of the cell.

NEWTON the BENJAMIN BANNEKER; physicist MICHAEL
(1642~1727) (1731~1806) (1791~1867)

scientists add to human knowledge. Those of GEORGE'S

era and in the years since built upon the work of the scientists who

preceded them, such as astronomers GALILEO, (1564~1642) ISAAC

Pierre Curie (1859~1906) and Marie Sklodowska CURIE (1867~1934)

Charles Darwin (1809~1882)

Edwin Hubble (1889~1953)

Annie Jump Cannon (1863~1941)

Louis Pasteur (1822-1895)

Alexander Fleming (1881-1955)

Albert Einstein (1879~1955)

Gregor Mendel (1822~1884)

Thomas Hunt Morgan (1860~1945)

Rachel Carson (1907~1964)

Ernest Everett Just (1883~1941)

Percy Julian (1899~1975)

TUSKEGEE TROUBLES

GEORGE ABSOLUTELY MADE CLOSE FRIENDS IN TUSKEGEE. Folks thereabouts would come to know him as a kindly neighbor, a generous teacher who visited with them on their porches or worked alongside them in their gardens, sharing what he knew about agriculture and nutrition. Unfortunately, some Tuskegeans saw him as an overpaid outsider from up North. In a land full of ugly attitudes about race, the fact that his skin was very dark added to whatever bad feelings folks might have about him. The way frugal George wore his clothes to tatters bugged some of his coworkers, too. Still, however shabby his jacket might be, a fresh flower always bloomed in its lapel.

He *was* uniquely smart, gifted, and well educated. Trouble was, sometimes George acted like he knew it. On top of that, he asked for not one, but *two* rooms for himself, his vast collection

1902

Beatrix Potter *writes and illustrates* The Tale of Peter Rabbit.

Alphonso XIII, *16, begins his reign as king of Spain, and U.S. troops pull out of independent Cuba. Bedouin warriors led by* **Abd al-Aziz ibn Saud** *begin the kingdom of Saudi Arabia.*

Feb. 1 —
Langston Hughes, *African-American poet, is born in Missouri.*

of scientific specimens, paintings, and who knew what all when other fellows had to bunk two to a room! (Truly, mice and moisture from a leaky roof ruined many of his carefully preserved and labeled plant specimens. Eventually, he sent some of his collection back to Iowa State. Much of it is now preserved in the New York Botanical Garden.) As for his laboratory, George and his new students scavenged for discarded jars, bottles, rubber tubing, and even hubcaps that could be made into necessary equipment.

Equipping the laboratory

1903

People are introduced to Harley-Davidson motorcycles, the Tour de France bicycle race, the World Series of baseball, and films that tell a story, such as **Edwin S. Porter's** The Great Train Robbery, 11 minutes long. People pay 5¢ to see it in nickelodeons, the first movie theaters.

May 23 – July 26 — **Dr. Horatio Nelson Jackson, Sewell Crocker,** Bud the dog, and a Winton automobile travel America (mostly unpaved) in the nation's first cross-country car trip.

George writes an angry letter.

In his first weeks at Tuskegee, George's state of mind seems to have been a perfect storm of mixed feelings and frustration with his new surroundings. He hadn't been there two months when he wrote this astonishing letter to the gentlemen on the institute's Finance Committee:

"You doubtless know that I came here solely for the benefit of my people....Moreover I do not expect to teach many years, but will quit as soon as I can trust my work to others, and engage in my brush work [his painting], which will be of great honor to our people showing to what we may attain along science, history, literature and art."

Workplaces being the way they are, it is extremely likely that this letter was passed around and discussed by George's coworkers. It certainly did not improve their opinion of the new guy. Fortunately for George, he seems to have eventually made peace with his place at Tuskegee.

1903

Marie Curie *is the first woman to win a Nobel Prize with her husband,* **Pierre,** *and* **A. H. Becquerel** *for their study of radioactivity. In 1911, Marie Curie will win another, for discovering radium and polonium.*

Dec. 17 — Kitty Hawk, NC — **Orville** *and* **Wilbur Wright** *of Dayton, OH, accomplish the first successful flight of a heavier-than-air machine.*

1904

South of Manchuria, Japanese ships attack those of Russia (see 1905). Meanwhile, Russians are finishing the 3,200-mile-long Trans-Siberian Railroad, the world's longest.

As for George, he really wasn't used to living in communities of black people. For the most part, he'd been raised and praised by whites. It wasn't until George was half grown that he ever even saw a large group of African Americans. They were, he wrote, "singers from Fisk," meaning the Jubilee Singers, organized in 1871 at Fisk University. This amazing choir and their pianist, Miss Ella Shepard, wowed audiences on both sides of the Atlantic Ocean, including young George Carver out in western Kansas.

The Jubilee Singers

1904

Work begins on the Panama Canal.

World's Fair-goers at St. Louis, MO, have their first tastes of iced tea, hamburgers, ice cream cones, cotton candy—and the summer Olympics.

Helen Keller, blind and deaf since she was a baby, graduates with honors from Radcliffe College.

London, England — **James Barrie** debuts his play, Peter Pan or, The Boy Who Would Not Grow Up.

George had always worked hard. Still, he was known to complain about all that BTW expected him to do when he first arrived in Alabama. George quickly found himself to be as long on duties and responsibilities as he was short on clerical help and hours in the day. Besides being a teacher and a scientist, George was also head of the institute's research and the agriculture departments, so he had to direct people, conduct meetings, write reports, and serve on committees. And it was part of his job to oversee the grounds and buildings, including making sure that the *sanitary closets* (toilets) were working! And, in his spare time, George was expected to manage the school's fields, pastures, orchard, barns and beehives, sheep, chickens, dairy cows, pigs, and other livestock. If those critters needed any medical help, that, too, was George's responsibility.

A few months after George arrived at Tuskegee, lawmakers decided to fund an agricultural experiment station there. In his laboratory, in his classroom, or out in the fields set aside for research, George looked for and talked about ways to make life better for folks who made their living from the land. This is how he explained it: "The primary idea in all of my work was to help the farmer and fill the poor man's dinner pail."

1905

Sarah B. Walker, a.k.a. **Madame C. J. Walker,** hair-care manufacturer, becomes the first black millionaire businesswoman.

Albert Einstein publishes his Theory of Relativity, revolutionary notions about space, time, and energy and how they relate to each other.

In his book The Jungle, **Upton Sinclair** exposes corruption in the U.S. meat-packing industry.

In one experiment, for instance, he and his students raised silkworms, and for their food, they planted 300 mulberry trees. Unfortunately, silk production proved to be too impractical. Demonstrating how paints could be made from river clay was more successful. Decades before organic farming became trendy, George showed how planting *legumes* (beans, peanuts, clover, peas, etc.) and *composting* (using rotted organic material as fertilizer) turned old dirt into rich soil. Someone sowing these "green manures" in one field after another, season by season, would have a more productive farm while avoiding costly chemical fertilizers. This practice is known as crop rotation.

Sharing this sort of information with struggling, set-in-their-ways farmers was a big part of Tuskegee's mission, so another part of George's job was to produce pamphlets such as Bulletin No. 5: *Cow Peas* (1905) or No. 24: *The Pickling and Curing of Meat in Hot Weather* (1912). To reach more isolated families, Tuskegee sent a "moveable school" around the countryside. George designed it. BTW named it after the Eastern banker who funded it, and in 1906, the Jesup Agricultural Wagon was loaded with charts and equipment, then hitched to a team of mules or horses that hauled it and George or an agent from the U.S.

1905   **1906**

Jan. 22 —
St. Petersburg, Russia —
Many Russians lead hard, hungry lives. When a peaceful crowd of them go to the czars' Winter Palace to beg for government reform, they're run down and shot by mounted soldiers with machine guns.

Aug. 9 —
President Theodore Roosevelt *helps the Russians and the Japanese end their war. For this he will become the first American to win the Nobel Prize for peace in 1906.*

Lee De Forest's *invention, the triode vacuum tube, amplifies sound and makes radio and television possible.*

Department of Agriculture (USDA) around from one village to another. Later on, of course, mules or horses were replaced as the moveable school rumbled along in shiny, gas-powered vehicles.

Whether he was talking to students, farm folks on their front porches, or, later on, to congressmen in Washington, D.C.,

Jesup Wagon

1906

The Iranians use their people power to force **Shah Muzaffar al-Din** to give them a constitution and a parliament.

Feb. 10 —
Arms race! Great Britain's HUGE new battleship Dreadnought inspires German **Emperor Wilhelm II** *to build bigger warships of his own.*

April 18 — 5:13 a.m. — Nearly 2,500 people die in San Francisco's terrible earthquake, followed by an equally terrible fire.

"Dr. Carver" had a knack for explaining. (Did GWC complete a Ph.D.? No, but folks had called him "Doctor" since his Iowa days. He'd correct them, but the title stuck. Later on, in 1928, George would receive an honorary doctoral degree from Simpson College, the school he'd attended in Indianola, Iowa.)

Visiting with neighbors

Problems? He had plenty with time, money, and some people. Whatever his difficulties in adapting to Tuskegee, George was a truly gifted educator. Booker T. Washington would criticize him for not reining in his restless mind, for jumping about "from one subject to another without regard to the course of study laid down in the catalogue." But BTW recognized in GWC "a great teacher, a great lecturer, a great inspirer of young men."

1907

The **Lumiere brothers** *invent a practical way of making color photographs.*

Frenchman **Paul Cornu** *makes the first free flight in a helicopter.*

1908

Robert Baden-Powell *of Great Britain starts the Boy Scouts.* **William Boyce** *will begin the American Boy Scouts in 1910.*

Henry Ford *introduces his Model T automobile.*

George and his "children"

George was, for the most part, popular with his students in spite of the fact that his subject was scientific agriculture. Most of them came from hardscrabble rural backgrounds. They saw their education as a ticket *off* the farm and *into* a life where they'd never have to think about agriculture, scientific or otherwise. Still, they

1908

Auburn, NY —
Former Civil War scout
Harriet Tubman,
who led slaves to freedom,
opens a home for poor
and elderly black folks.

Kenneth Grahame
publishes The Wind
in the Willows.

Aug. 27 —
President **Lyndon Baines
Johnson** *is born in Texas.*

Nov. 3 —
The 27th U.S. President will
be **William Howard Taft.**

responded to George's jokes, his obvious enthusiasm, and the way he wove different sciences into his presentations. A lesson about growing the Ipomoea batatas (sweet potato) might include botany, chemistry, and nutrition, as well as the effects of *meteorology* (weather), *ecology* (how living things relate to one another and to their environment), *pedology* (soil), and *entomology* (insects).

George believed that "a very large part of a child's education must be gotten outside of the four walls designated as class room." So, off they would go, George and "his children," as he called his students, on hikes, field trips, and specimen hunts. He guided them in seeing that all of nature was interconnected; it was one. He pushed them to think for themselves.

"This old notion of swallowing down other people's ideas and problems just as they've worked them out, without putting our brain and originality into it, and making them applicable to our specific [needs] must go," George wrote. "And the sooner we let them go the sooner we will be a free and independent people."

In the first decade of the 20th century, African Americans' yearning for true freedom, equality, and independence was more powerful than ever.

1908

1909

Dec. 26 —
Boxer **Jack Johnson** *becomes the first black American to be the world's heavyweight champion.*

Count Ferdinand von Zeppelin, *airship pioneer, helps to start the first commercial airline.*

April 6 —
Explorers **Robert E. Peary,** *African American* **Matthew Henson,** *and four Inuit, a.k.a. Eskimos, men are the first to reach the North Pole.*

A RUSHING TORRENT OF PROTEST

Just about everyone agreed with Booker T. Washington's belief that African Americans should stick together and help themselves by learning trades and working hard. But many blacks bitterly disagreed with his notion that blacks should back off from their dreams of full equality and put up with a world run by whites. BTW's most important critic was history professor Dr. William Edward Burghardt Du Bois. He declared that all blacks must take pride in their race, protest prejudice, and fight for full equality. To that end, he and 29 other professors, ministers, teachers, newspaper editors, and lawyers met near Niagara Falls in July 1905. W.E.B. Du Bois led the "Niagara Movement" until 1910, when it merged into the National Association for the Advancement of Colored People (NAACP).

1910

President Taft *throws out the first ball of the season and starts a big-league baseball tradition.*

Showman **Florenz Ziegfeld** *hires African-American performer* **Bert Williams,** *who becomes a Broadway star in the famous Ziegfeld Follies.*

*Paris, France —
Inventor* **Georges Claude** *shows off the first electric neon light.*

THE PRINCIPAL

IN THE 25 YEARS BEFORE GEORGE CAME TO THE Tuskegee Institute, Booker T. Washington had been building up his school. After GWC arrived in 1896, BTW kept on writing, giving speeches, drumming up donations, and organizing political support for his school. He never stopped trying to coax decent treatment for his people out of the stubborn, racist establishment. He involved himself in the National Negro Business League he started in 1900, and he ran and/or supported newspapers for blacks. All the while he tried to keep things harmonious between the overworked, stressed-out teachers — including brilliant, temperamental GWC — and his cash-strapped institute.

Booker T. Washington towered over the school he founded. When the man George had totally admired became sick and died on November 14, 1915, he was in despair. What now?

1910

After a successful rebellion against **Porfirio Diaz's** dictatorship, **Francisco "Pancho" Villa** and **Emiliano Zapata** struggle for control of Mexico (see 1916).

May 6 — **King Edward VII** is dead. Long live **George V** of Great Britain, cousin of both **Nicholas II,** czar of Russia, and Germany's **Emperor Wilhelm II.**

1911

Ernest Rutherford, discoverer of protons and alpha and beta rays, considers the structure of atoms. Other physicists, particularly **Niels Bohr** and **Max Planck,** will build on his work.

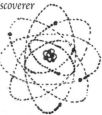

"May God help each boy and girl, man and woman to catch the vision of his own destiny." G.W.C. 1929

each one is an architect of his own fortune, the carver... of his own... opportunity...for indeed

CHAPTER FIVE

THE SAGE OF TUSKEGEE

INTO THE LIGHT

IN THE YEARS AFTER BOOKER T. WASHINGTON DIED in 1915, more and more people, black and white, began to take notice of George Washington Carver. He came out of the long shadow cast by Tuskegee's founder. More and more, he was speaking to white as well as black audiences at colleges and conferences, around the country. Traveling wasn't easy, by the way, considering all of the hotels, restaurants, and railroad sleeping cars that were closed to him because of the color of his skin. Once George was asked to use a freight elevator instead of riding up with the white folks who were on their way to hear him give a speech.

1911

High on a Peruvian mountain, U.S. explorer **Hiram Bingham** finds the ruins of the ancient Inca city of Machu-Picchu.

Feb. 6 — President **Ronald Reagan** is born in Illinois.

March 25 — Fire in New York City's Triangle shirtwaist factory kills 146 people, mostly young women, in smoke, flames, or desperate jumps.

Dec. 14 — **Roald Amundsen** of Norway discovers the South Pole. Englishman **Robert F. Scott** and four other explorers got there a few weeks later; all five died of cold and hunger on their return trek.

When he spoke, folks would be taken aback at first by his oddly high-pitched voice. Soon, though, they were captivated by the stories charismatic George wove into his talks about "Worn Out Soils" or "Scientific Agriculture." To a listener in one of his audiences, George's deep black eyes seemed "to have two gleaming coals of living fire behind them. His skin is extremely dark, but when he begins to talk, race and color are lost sight of and one hears a wonderfully soft, musical voice telling a story...."

People visited with George at fairs, where he'd preside over an exhibit (artistically arranged) of every sort of product a creative chemist could devise from anything grown or gotten from the land. A substitute for rubber made from sweet potatoes? He was working on it. Plastic from soybeans? Milk made from peanuts? Absolutely. In 1918, George shared his peanut milk recipe with a medical missionary working in Africa's Belgian Congo (present-day Democratic Republic of the Congo). Those who kept cows in that part of Africa didn't keep them long, thanks to hungry lions and disease-carrying tsetse flies. For children who needed milk, George's non-dairy variety was a lifesaver.

In 1916, George got his name in America's newspapers. Not only did the National Agricultural Society ask for his official

1912

Hans Geiger *invents the Geiger counter to detect radioactive elements.*	*Polish chemist* **Casimir Funk** *comes up with the concept and the word "vitamin."*	*After 267 years, the Manchu dynasty falls, and China becomes a republic. Its last emperor, 6-year-old* **Puyi,** *no longer has the power to rule.*	*March 12 — Savannah, GA —* **Juliette Gordon "Daisy" Low** *begins the American Girl Scouts.*
Maria Montessori *publishes her teaching methods.*			

advice, but Great Britain's Royal Society for the Encouragement of Arts also invited him to be a member. These honors made the public more aware of the research being done by a scientist who started out in life as an enslaved, kidnapped, orphaned, sick baby, traded for a $300 horse (Moses Carver's reward to George's rescuer). George, with his dramatic life story and unique personality, had the makings of a popular hero. In the 1920s and the tough economic times of the 1930s, he caught the attention of the U.S. Government, the admiration of a titan of industry, and the imagination of the American people.

WAR

IN THE SUMMER OF 1914, George was bruised and banged up in an automobile accident, but, as he reported in a letter to his old friends, the Milhollands, he had "no bones broken." Over in

1912

April 14 – 15 —
A collision with an iceberg sends the great oceanliner Titanic *and nearly 1,500 of her passengers down to the bottom of the Atlantic Ocean.*

April 16 —
U.S. journalist/ aviator **Harriet Quimby** *is the first woman to fly across the English Channel.*

Nov. 5 —
In the U.S. election, Democrat **Woodrow Wilson** *defeats* **President William H. Taft** *and third party candidate* **Theodore Roosevelt.**

Submarine

Europe that same summer, an entire way of life was getting smashed in a collision of world powers: The Great War, a.k.a. World War I (WWI), had begun. Great Britain, France, and their Allies fought Germany, Bulgaria, and Austria-Hungary, as well as the Ottoman Empire, which, along with the fighting, extended across Turkey into Mesopotamia (now known as Iraq) and the lands of the Middle East. By April 1917, after German *U-boats* (submarines) sank a few too many U.S. merchant ships, America jumped into the fight, siding with the Allies.

Huge government-sponsored advertising campaigns urged civilians to cut back on foods needed to feed soldiers. The U.S. Food Administrator and future President Herbert Hoover called for "wheatless" Mondays and Wednesdays as well as "meatless" Tuesdays. You can be sure that these campaigns brought more publicity to George, author of Tuskegee Bulletin No. 36. *How to Make Sweet Potato Flour, Starch, Sugar, Bread, and Mock Cocoanut* (1918).

The war effort inspired hunts for more than sweet potato bread. Military researchers experimented with flamethrower

1913

Jan. 9 —
President **Richard Nixon** *is born in California.*

Feb. 4 —
Civil rights activist **Rosa Lee Parks** *is born in Alabama.*

July 14 —
Leslie King, a.k.a. President **Gerald Ford***, is born in Nebraska.*

Dec. 21 —
The first crossword puzzle in a U.S. newspaper is printed in the New York Sunday World.

tanks and wireless communication on the battlefield. Thomas Edison, now 70 years old, worked on underwater listening devices. The airplane, developed by the Wright brothers among others, fought by the thousands, swarming and swooping high over Europe's muddy, bloody battlefields. Early in the war, pilots fired pistols at one another. Air battles became more effective (deadly) once aviators figured out how to use machine guns without shooting off their propellers.

Despite the horrible way their countrymen had treated them, some 300,000 African-American troops served their

Dogfight!

1914

Irish explorer **Ernest H. Shackleton** begins an ill-fated, 3-year expedition to Antarctica.

A big event in the history of American blues and jazz: black bandleader/composer **W.C. Handy** publishes his "St. Louis Blues."

June 28 — A political shooting in Sarajevo, Bosnia, sparks a summer of troubles, four years of World War I, and a century of after-effects (see 1919).

country in WWI. They had to put up with jeering, disrespect, and bad training. Most were given necessary but dirty, menial jobs behind the lines. Still, those who fought did it bravely. Blacks hoped that military service would win some respect for their race, but no. Seventy were lynched in 1919 when the troops came home, including 10 black veterans in uniform. At least 20 U.S. cities were hit with race riots, as tough economic times inflamed ugly attitudes.

Particularly in America's big manufacturing and meatpacking towns, such as Pittsburgh, Pennsylvania, Detroit, Michigan, and Chicago, Illinois, WWI veterans, regardless of race, competed for jobs with multitudes of new arrivals from famine-blighted Eastern Europe and from the American South. Between 1910 and 1930, nearly a million black Americans moved north in a Great Migration. All of the work of Tuskegee and other schools like it, all of George's lessons about self-reliance and careful, creative farming — these could not overcome plagues of *boll weevils* (cotton-devouring beetles) and centuries of pure and wretched meanness. In the words of a Mississippi sharecropper's daughter and future civil rights activist Fannie Lou Hamer (1917–1977), southern blacks were "sick and tired of being sick and tired."

1914   **1915**

Aug. 3 — The Panama Canal opens to ship traffic.	**D. W. Griffith** *makes the first major motion picture. Despite some racist scenes, Birth of a Nation shows what an awesome art form movies can be.*	*The long-shut-down Ku Klux Klan begins officially reorganizing. Besides terrorizing blacks, its members also target "un-American" immigrants, Jews, and Roman Catholics.*		Jan. 25 — **Alexander Graham Bell** *makes the first transcontinental telephone connection—to whom? None other than* **Thomas A. Watson,** *the first man who ever answered a phone, March 10, 1876.*

FAME

🦋

IN 1921, MR. CARVER WENT TO WASHINGTON. Lawmakers in the House of Representatives Ways and Means Committee were considering a *tariff* (a tax) on peanuts coming in from China. Getting an expert to come testify was and is an old congressional custom. Being advised by a black citizen was not at all customary in the early 20th century, but George knew peanuts. He knew some big shots, too, such as peanut businessmen who'd enjoyed his informative speeches about this tasty legume. And he was well acquainted with not one but two Cabinet officials. James Wilson, the Secretary of Agriculture for Presidents McKinley, T. Roosevelt, and William H. Taft, once taught at Iowa State. So had the current man on the job, Henry C. Wallace. His son used to go on nature walks with George back in 1894, when GWC was an instructor and little Henry, Jr., was six.

1915

Jan. 28 —
Congress establishes the
U.S. Coast Guard.

April 22 — France —
German forces begin using
poison chlorine gas as a
battlefield weapon.

May 7 —
German submarine sinks the
Lusitania, a British oceanliner,
killing 1,198 passengers, including
128 Americans (see 1917).

"THE NEW NEGRO":
THE HARLEM RENAISSANCE,
AND OTHER VOICES

Southern blacks as well as islanders from the West Indies poured into Detroit, Chicago, Cleveland, and other big cities of the North. Over the years as folks settled in New York City's Harlem section, its population went from 152,500 in 1920 to 327,700 in 1930. As a vibrant culture blossomed, the time and place became known as the Harlem Renaissance. The era crackled and sparkled with the sculpture of Augusta Savage, the paintings of Palmer Hayden, and the musical comedy of Eubie Blake, among others. Claude McKay and Langston Hughes were two of many outstanding black writers. Dancers twirled and stomped "The Lindy Hop," "The Black Bottom," and "the Big Apple" to the music of W.C. Handy, Louis Armstrong, and Edward K. "Duke" Ellington or to that of Ferdinand "Jelly Roll" Morton. While crowds in Paris, France, were going bananas over entertainer Josephine Baker,

American audiences cried and laughed (in a good way) at such performers as Paul Robeson, Ethel Waters, and Bert Williams. Still, for all of their tremendous talents, none of these artists could ever entirely escape rude and unequal treatment.

Blacks found comfort and courage in their churches, societies, lodges, self-help organizations, marching bands, and choirs. They took heart as they sang "Lift Every Voice and Sing," an anthem composed by brothers J. Rosamond and James Weldon Johnson. Marcus Garvey's campaign for an African homeland for black Americans ultimately failed, but this gifted black orator lifted his people's pride in their race. They were proud, too, of businesswoman Madame C. J. Walker. Her beauty products empire made her a millionaire, a first for black women. Long before Jackie Robinson joined the Brooklyn Dodgers in 1947 and white baseball began to be integrated, black teams such as Pennsylvania's Homestead Grays, the Baltimore Black Sox, and the Kansas City Monarchs played terrific baseball. Their cheering fans filled the stands.

That little boy grew up to be Agriculture Secretary (1933–40) then Vice President (1940–44) under FDR (President Franklin D. Roosevelt, 1933–1945).

In the summer of 1921, 39-year-old FDR was stricken with poliomyelitis and was fighting for his life. Someday, George would make headlines for his method of helping "polio" patients. For now, though, it was 1921, and there was George in a rumpled old suit with a flower in his lapel getting ready to show powerful politicians the peanut's possibilities.

"All right, Mr. Carver," said the Chairman, a representative from the state of Michigan. "We will give you ten minutes."

As he had in many a classroom and county fair, George laid out containers of milk, buttermilk, instant coffee, candies, livestock foods, and dyes, then taught and explained how all of these products had been made from peanuts.

"Here is a breakfast food," said George. "I am very sorry that you cannot taste this, so I will taste it for you."

The congressmen chuckled as he took a bite. The presentation went so well that when the scheduled ten minutes were up, the Chairman said, "Go ahead, brother. Your time is unlimited."

So dignified, crowd-pleasing George went on testifying

1916

*No one had ever demonstrated outside the White House until **Alice Paul** and other suffragists begin picketing, demanding women's right to vote. They're arrested, jailed, and mistreated (see 1920).*

March 9 — **Pancho Villa** *leads a deadly raid on a New Mexico town.* **President Wilson** *sends soldiers south to capture Villa. They never do.*

Oct. 16 — **Margaret Sanger** *is arrested and jailed for opening a birth control clinic in Brooklyn, NY.*

for nearly an hour. In newspapers across the land, Americans would read about the scientist from Tuskegee. Even the great Thomas Edison seemed to know enough about him to offer him a job as a scientific researcher, so the story goes, with a big fat paycheck, but no. George was to stay in Alabama.

Mr. Carver goes to Washington

And he was to be famous for the rest of his life.

Fame did not mean personal riches, but George, who was known to forget all about uncashed paychecks he had stuffed in his desk, had no interest in becoming a rich man. Besides, he

1917

Russia —
The outbreak of the Bolshevik revolution ends 350 years of czarist rule (see 1918). Out of all of the violence, the Soviet Union will rise, lasting until 1991. Fear of Russian-style communism sparks a "Red Scare" in the U.S. where thousands of citizens and immigrants are arrested in the next few years.

In Chicago, the Original Dixieland Jass (spelling changed later on!) Band makes the first jazz recordings.

May 29 —
President **John Fitzgerald Kennedy** is born in Massachusetts.

PEANUT MAN

South Americans knew about peanuts centuries before Portuguese sailors brought the plants to Europe in the 16th century. Peanuts (*arachis hypogea*) aren't nuts at all; they're part of the pea family. Still, they've attracted some pretty nutty nicknames — goobers, goober peas, groundnuts (because they grow under the soil's surface) even monkey nuts! When Tuskegee published Bulletin No. 31 in 1916, George gave this 20-page pamphlet a snappy title: *How to Grow the Peanut and 105 Ways of Preparing it for Human Consumption.* No. 51 was a recipe for Peanut Butter. George did not claim to invent it, and truly, the process for the kind of smooth *hydrogenated* (oil made nicely solid by adding hydrogen) peanut butter we're used to was developed around 1923 by J. L. Rosefield, the genius who came up with chunky peanut butter.

Eventually GWC came up with almost 300 ways to use the peanut, including printers' ink, house paint, milk substitutes, and cosmetics. Peanut oil is still used to keep machines running smoothly, and it's found in everything from shampoo to nitroglycerin. Manufacturers grind up peanut shells and use them in such things as plastics, wallboard, and abrasives for polishing and scrubbing.

Peanut Pods

Tap Root

Secondary Roots

didn't have much talent for business or manufacturing. Still, in the 1920s and 1930s, George was happy — more or less — to advise those who were more commercially inclined.

In the head office of the Ralston-Purina Company, there was interest in those breakfast foods George told the congressmen about, but it never worked out. Grocery shoppers wouldn't be buying bright boxes of Carvo-Puffs or Goober-Flakes.

George and his colleagues at the institute, along with men from the town of Tuskegee, drummed up a handful of short-lived businesses designed to manufacture products based on his research. Soon, George could send letters to friends on stationery with "Carver Products Company, Inc." on the letterhead. He got a bang out of that and out of sharing glorious news. In 1923, the Atlanta, Georgia, chapter of the United Daughters of the Confederacy sent George word of their official appreciation of his work. What's more, the NAACP awarded him their coveted prize for merit. Only the most distinguished African Americans, such as biologist Ernest E. Just in 1915, or W.E.B. Du Bois in 1920 (Oprah Winfrey in 2000), received the annual Spingarn Medal, named after civil rights leader/educator Joel Spingarn.

Despite George's good publicity, the Carver Products

1917

April 2 — **President Woodrow Wilson** asks Congress to declare war on Germany.

July 10 — **Don Herbert**, a.k.a. "Mr. Wizard," is born in Minnesota. In the 1950s–60s, he'll teach science to children on his popular TV program.

1918

Author/illustrator **Johnny Gruelle** invents the doll Raggedy Ann.

Flu Pandemic! This year and next, 20 to 40 million people around the world die of influenza.

Company, Inc. and two more ventures connected with him struggled and ultimately fizzled out. Out of these enterprises came three patented manufacturing methods (two for paint processes, one for peanut-based cosmetics). A product called Penol actually made it to drugstore shelves in the 1920s. George developed it with peanuts and *creosote* (a product made from wood tar that used to be a common ingredient in respiratory remedies). George had high hopes that Penol would help people with tuberculosis, the dreaded lung disease. He said so, too, in a speech on November 18, 1924, to a big crowd of people in a grand old church in New York City. And that's not all; George went on to share with the audience the way he worked in his research laboratory.

"I never have to grope for methods; the method is revealed at the moment I am inspired to create something new," said Tuskegee's renowned chemist. Divine revelation was a big part of the way he operated.

When he finished speaking, George was rewarded with smiles and applause, but he hadn't won everybody's heart that night. A *New York Times* reporter went back to the office, wrote an editorial about Tuskegee's renowned chemist, and called it

---

1918

April 21 —
Famed German flying ace **"Red Baron" Manfred von Richthofen,** *credited with shooting down 80 enemy airplanes, is mortally wounded in his red, triple-winged Fokker.*

July 16 —
Bolsheviks kill Russia's last royal family: **Czar Nicholas II,** *his wife* **Alexandra,** *and children,* **Olga, Tatiana, Marie, Anastasia,** *and* **Alexis.**

Nov. 11 —
Armistice Day: At the 11th hour on the 11th day of the 11th month, the guns of WWI fall silent.

"Men of Science Never Talk That Way." Where was George's "scientific spirit?" Real chemists drew upon scientific knowledge recorded in books. They did not, as George did, chalk up their successes to "inspiration" or to "Mr. Creator" drawing back the curtain to reveal the answers.

"Talk of that sort," the writer continued, "simply will bring ridicule on an admirable institution [Tuskegee] and on the race for which it has done and still is doing so much."

In response to those stinging words, George whipped out a long reply loaded with Bible verses and lists of where he'd studied and science books he'd read. "The more information one has," he wrote, "the greater will be the inspiration."

His letter wasn't printed in the *New York Times*, but folks read it in other papers and rushed to write letters of their own in support of George. He took heart from the many people who took his part in this squabble. His confidence was boosted by invitations to speak here and there around the U.S. Out on the road, George put up with inconveniences, such as having to sit up all night on a jouncing train and sleep as best he could since there was no sleeping car for those whose souls were contained in dark skin. In between his travels and writing, he returned to

1919

Could a rocket fly to the moon? Scientist **Robert H. Goddard** tells how in his report, A Method of Reaching Extreme Altitudes (*see 1926*).

Inventor **George B. Hansburg** patents his pogo stick.

June 28 — France — *WWI officially ends when the Treaty of Versailles is signed. Besides all of the wounded, missing, and lives otherwise broken, more than 14 million soldiers and civilians are dead.*

an old interest: doing some valuable research into fungus-caused diseases that attacked peanut plants. In this way, George kept busy throughout the 1920s and into the 1930s, when he again made the news and an important friend.

A CRIPPLED NATION

SINCE ANCIENT TIMES PEOPLE HAVE BEEN TERRIFIED of the paralyzing illness we know as polio. Because it seemed to strike young people, it came to be known as infantile poliomyelitis. The discovery in 1908 that the disease was caused by a virus didn't make it any less scary. It seemed to come like a sudden storm, overtaking unsuspecting, healthy people, leaving them in pain and unable to move. Not until 1955 would polio be controlled by Dr. Jonas Salk's vaccine. More than 20 years earlier, George was doing his best to get polio's victims back on their feet.

1920

Jan. 16 —
Prohibition goes into effect. By last year's Act of Congress, U.S. citizens may not make, buy, or sell alcoholic beverages (see 1933).

Aug. 26 —
At last! The 19th Amendment is ratified. Female citizens of the U.S. are allowed to vote.

Nov. 2 —
The nation's first commercial radio broadcast is out of KDKA, Pittsburgh, PA. Listeners hear the election news: Republican **Warren G. Harding** *will be the next U.S. President.*

Since the 1890s, when he rubbed the aching backs of Iowa football athletes, George had been giving massages. Between his strong hands, his sensitivity, and his scientific training, George was good at helping folks feel better. Being curious, he won-

Children challenged by polio

dered what would happen if he rubbed nutritious peanut oil into muscles affected by polio? Sure enough, in 1933 when George tried his theory on a couple of patients, they saw genuine improvement in muscle strength and blood circulation. Being truly enthusiastic about helping "suffering humanity" and being unabashedly fond of publicity, George was quick to tell people, including a reporter for the Associated Press, his good results.

Had Dr. Carver found a cure? No, but such news surely would have been thrilling in an awfully bleak time. In the 1930s, folks badly needed cheering up. Nearly 13 million Americans, a fourth of the U.S. population, were out of work thanks to the

1920

James Weldon Johnson, *African-American poet and diplomat, becomes general secretary of the NAACP.*

1921

June 30 —
William H. Taft *becomes the only ex-President to serve as Chief Justice of the Supreme Court.*

1922

Benito Mussolini *becomes dictator of Italy. Under his strict, hyper-patriotic, fascist government, citizens have few freedoms. But, unlike in Russia where property was controlled by the communist government, they may own their businesses.*

Depression (a huge economic slump; see time line, 1929). As hard times spread around the world, folks went broke. They lost their homes and farms. Such trouble and fear gave rise to military dictatorships in Japan, Italy, and Germany.

Jobless, homeless Americans hit the road.

Meanwhile, hopeful Americans scooped bottles of peanut oil from store shelves. Sacks full of mail and cars full of suffering humans showed up at the institute. Everyone wanted help from — or just wished to glimpse — the man known as the "Goober Wizard" or the "Peanut Man." George was also called the "Black Burbank," after horticulturist Luther Burbank, and even the

1922

U.S. inventor **Philo T. Farnsworth** *advances TV technology with his electronic scanning system (see 1926).*

Canada —
Researchers **Frederick G. Banting** *and* **Charles H. Best** *pioneer the use of insulin to treat diabetes.*

Nov. 26 —
Egypt —
Howard Carter *discovers the treasure-filled tomb of Tutankhamun, a.k.a.* **King Tut.**

"Black Leonardo," after Da Vinci, the multi-gifted Italian artist.

George took on a few clients, never charging a fee. In person or in letters, he advised polio sufferers to see a doctor, exercise their withered muscles, rub them with peanut oil, and bathe in hot salt water. His treatments never received official endorsement from the medical profession, and it's likely that George's peanut oil was not as helpful as the rubbing that went with it. His methods (minus the peanut oil) were similar to those that would be made famous in the early 1940s by Australian nurse Elizabeth Kenny. The fact that George was poor at recording his notes and formulas did not help this or any of his causes, but he really did help quite a few people regain strength and movement.

A polio rehabilitation clinic for blacks was built at Tuskegee, thanks to George's efforts and a bit of pressure from Franklin D. Roosevelt. FDR became an expert on ways to help folks crippled with polio after it robbed him of the use of his legs. As President, FDR combined southern campaigning with treatment at the clinic he founded at Warm Springs, Georgia, not too far from the institute. So it was that he came to Tuskegee in 1939. FDR and GWC shook hands as an equally joyous crowd of Tuskegeans clustered around the President's open car.

1923

Frank C. Mars *comes up with the Milky Way candy bar. His company will introduce Snickers in 1930.*

Aug. 2 – 3 — **Warren G. Harding** *dies. His* **Vice President Calvin Coolidge** *becomes the 30th U.S. President.*

1924

American explorer **Roy C. Andrews,** *fossil-hunting in Asia's Gobi Desert, finds skeletons of dinosaurs and— a first—their eggs!*

GOLD OUT OF STRAW, PLASTIC OUT OF BEANS

IN 1933, AMERICANS TUNED THEIR AM DIALS to listen to Franklin Roosevelt explain his policies on the radio, a presidential first. His aristocratic voice cut through the static. As of this year, folks would be able to get better reception thanks to *frequency modulation* (FM), developed by Edwin H. Armstrong, 43. Vladimir K. Zworykin, 44, and Philo T. Farnsworth, 27, were bringing the world ever closer to electronic television. And at the world's fair in Chicago this year visitors saw many things, but plastics made from soybeans? Most people had never heard of such a thing.

The scientist who conjured plastic out of plants was part of an industrial trend known as chemurgy (KEHM-ur-jee). So was George. He'd been a chemurgist long before American chemist

1924

Kimberly & Clark company chemist **Ernst Mahler** invents disposable handkerchiefs, known as Kleenex.

Jan. 21 — Russian revolutionary leader **V. I. Lenin** dies. **Joseph Stalin** gathers power (see 1929).

Nov. 30 — RCA (Radio Corporation of America) sends moving images over the air waves, from London to New York City.

1925

Marcus Garvey heads more than 700 branches of his Universal Negro Improvement Association (see page 101).

Listening to FDR on the radio

William J. Hale came up with the concept in 1935. The word never really caught on. Now people say biochemical engineering. It just means using plants as raw materials for chemical manufacturing. For instance, in 1932, George worked on turning cotton fibers into road paving material. He was delighted at the prospect of corn, barley, and other field cops being transformed into "power alcohol." George saw such bio-fuels as a way people could adjust as Earth's petroleum deposits ran dry. He envisioned a day when "out of the soil, we will make our houses, our clothes, our automobiles — everything on earth we need. Plant chemistry is just at its beginnings. We have only opened a crack in the door. "If," George continued, "wars are caused by the lack

1925

Where there's fast music, dancers dance the Charleston.

July 10 – 21 — Dayton, TN —
*Americans eat up every detail of **John T. Scopes**'s "Monkey Trial." He's tried, convicted, and fined $100 for teaching the theory of evolution in his high school biology class. Defending him is **Clarence Darrow**, hired by the 5-year-old American Civil Liberties Union. The prosecutor is famous politician/orator **William Jennings Bryan**.*

*May 19 — Malcolm Little, a.k.a. **Malcolm X**, African-American leader, is born in Nebraska.*

George

of things there will be no more wars because the earth will pour forth plenty for everybody."

That kind of thinking totally fascinated inventor/manufacturer/auto industry tycoon Henry Ford. Millions of his affordable, mass-produced Model Ts (see time line, 1908) were transforming American life, including the lives of blacks. They not only drove Ford automobiles. They helped to build them. Henry's company was the first to hire blacks in significant numbers, and he paid them the same as he paid his white workers. He was aiming his attention at finding creative uses for farm products. After all, how could farmers buy cars if they didn't have customers to buy their crops? Those soybean plastics at the 1933 Chicago fair were knobs, handles, and buttons developed by Robert Boyer, a

1925

Aug. 8 —
*Washington, DC —
At least 40,000 Ku Klux Klan members march through the streets of the nation's capital.*

1926

A. A. Milne
writes Winnie-the-Pooh.

*American scientist **Thomas Hunt Morgan** tells in his Theory of the Gene how characteristics are passed from one generation to the next.*

*Scottish engineer **John Logie Baird** comes up with a TV system based on infrared rays (see 1929).*

chemical engineer on Ford's payroll, made for Ford automobiles.

Henry

It was their shared interest that brought George and Henry together at a chemurgic conference in Michigan in 1937. Newspapers recorded a sad, curious incident that happened there. Though he'd been invited, George skipped the big banquet, choosing to eat in his room. He waited outside the noisy ballroom until it was time for him to give his talk. Only then did he take his place at the head table with Henry Ford and the other speakers. Why? Perhaps, after decades of segregation, George felt that he, along with everyone else, would be more at ease dining separately. It might've been a way of being special, or maybe frail, 72-year-old George simply preferred privacy when his coffee cup sloshed in his trembling hand.

1926   **1927**

March 16 —
Auburn, MA —
Robert H. Goddard *sends the first liquid-fuel rocket 184 feet into the air.*

April 21 —
Elizabeth Alexandra Mary Windsor, *present-day queen of the United Kingdom, is born in London, England.*

Oct. 18 —
Chuck Berry, *musician, is born in Missouri.*

Movies speak! They'd been silent, actors' words printed on the screen, until this year's The Jazz Singer.

In any case, George, the Tuskegee chemist, and Henry, the Detroit tycoon, struck up an unlikely friendship. Each admired the other's creativity, and when it came to creative genius, theirs was a case of "takes one to know one." More than once they visited each another, photographers snapping their pictures for the newspapers. On his estate in Georgia, Henry founded a George Washington Carver School. Later, when George's health began to fail, Henry had an elevator installed so his fragile friend could get upstairs in his Tuskegee dormitory.

In the last years of his life, white-haired, stooped-shouldered, sick and shaky old George set his heart on a place where all of his paintings and experiments could be displayed. Before he died — and it wouldn't be long now, he knew — he wanted people to be able to come and, as he put it, "catch the vision" of all that he'd done and tried to do. He dreamed of a laboratory where young black scientists could do research. He wanted all of this so badly that he donated all of his savings to the project — nearly $60,000! His old Michigan friend, 77-year-old Henry Ford, donated money as well and came to Tuskegee for the dedication of George's museum in 1941. Considering all of the time young George had spent with washtubs and clotheslines, it

1927

Jazz composer, pianist **Edward Kennedy "Duke" Ellington,** 28, and his band begin playing at the Cotton Club in the Harlem section of New York, NY.

May 10 — Chicago, IL — Trumpeter **Louis "Satchmo" Armstrong** and his band record "The Potato Head Blues."

LOUIS ARMSTRONG

May 20 – 21 — **Charles A. Lindbergh,** 25, takes off from New York. When he lands near Paris, 33.5 hours later, he's instantly totally famous, the first pilot to fly solo, non-stop, across the Atlantic Ocean (see 1932).

George's museum

was somehow fitting that his museum was housed in what used to be Tuskegee's laundry building.

Later that year, when Henry's employees created a steel-framed car with a cream-colored body made of sturdy, gleaming plant-based plastic, George delighted in his friend's technological triumph. Only months later, Henry would turn away from chemurgy-on-wheels, and George would return to thinking about food as he had back in World War I. Why? Because a second, even more terrible war was beginning. America joined the fight, and the old friends wanted to help their country win it.

1928

Alexander Fleming
*of Great Britain
discovers* penicillin,
*the first antibiotic
for treating all sorts
of serious diseases.*

Walt Disney
*makes his first
Mickey Mouse
cartoons.*

1929

*Russian-born American
scientist* **Vladimir K.
Zworykin** *uses his
iconoscope and kinescope
to demonstrate the first
practical television system.*

WAR: THE SEQUEL

❧

IT WOULD TAKE A FAR BIGGER BOOK THAN THIS to explain WWII, but it boils down to this: The way WWI ended in 1918–19 left defeated Germany really wrecked, making it possible for a bitter,

Adolf Hitler

hyper-nationalistic bunch of power-grabbers like Adolf Hitler and his political followers take over the country. Then Germany, as well as hyper-military Japan and Italy began grabbing territory. After a few years of expanding nightmare in Europe and Asia, Japanese forces attacked the U.S. base at Pearl Harbor,

1929

Russian **Joseph Stalin** now heads the Union of Soviet Socialist Republics (*USSR, a.k.a. Soviet Union*). Millions will die of hunger and/or in prison during his fearsome dictatorship.

Jan. 15 —
Martin Luther King, Jr., *minister, civil rights leader, is born in Georgia.*

Oct. 24 – 28 —
The U.S. stock market crashes, causing all sorts of investors to lose billions of dollars. Panic spreads. The Great Depression is beginning.

Hawai'i, and the United States entered the war. By the time WWII ended in 1945, countless millions would be dead, including — well, more about that later (see time lines, 1939–1945).

Besides worrying about their loved ones fighting overseas, Americans were focused on supporting the war effort on the home front. Among other things, that meant conserving food and raising it, too. So, despite his various illnesses, George worked on his last Tuskegee Bulletin, No. 43: *Nature's Garden for Victory and Peace.* His right hand was too shaky, so he dictated the words for a leaflet *Peanuts to Conserve Meat.* Maybe, when he looked out the window from time to time, he might have caught sight of some particularly dashing young men.

African-American men came from all over the nation to Tuskegee, Alabama, to be part of the first black military pilot training unit in the U.S. armed forces. Between 1942 and 1946, 994 aviation cadets earned their silver wings by going through nine hard months of training. Then, as officers in the U. S. Army Air Corps, they were pilots, navigators, or bombardiers. Plenty of enlisted men trained as mechanics, parachute riggers, control tower operators, or took on other sorts of technical support. In the air or on the ground, blacks participating in military aviation

1930

Chicago, IL — Baker **James Dewar** *invents* Twinkies.

American inventor **Vannevar Bush** *devises a "differential analyzer," an ancestor of modern computers, and* **Ernest O. Lawrence** *is developing the cyclotron, an essential tool for splitting the atom (see 1942).*

Annie Jump Cannon, *"Census Taker of the Sky," has catalogued 400,000 stars.*

119

Tuskegee Airmen

1931

Black bandleader **Cab Calloway** records his hit song "Minnie the Moocher."

Pearl S. Buck *writes a bestseller,* The Good Earth.

1932

Oct. 18 — **Thomas A. Edison** *dies at age 84.*

English physicist **James Chadwick** *discovers the neutron, part of an atom's nucleus (center) with no electrical charge, unlike the positive proton or negative electron.*

was new. One thing had not changed, though. Like those who had taken part in earlier wars, the airmen from Tuskegee, as well as the hundreds of thousands of other blacks who served in WWII, had to put up with humiliating, racist attitudes from their fellow Americans — as if the Germans and the Japanese weren't trouble enough.

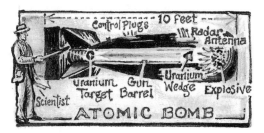

A Peaceful Life in a Perilous World

WHEN PEACEABLE GEORGE CAME INTO THE WORLD, the American Civil War was staggering to its end. When he left it, more than 50 nations were fighting a war even more terrible. The 78-or-so years between his beginning and end were absolutely peppered with new contraptions, technologies, and new understandings of how atoms, rays, and chromosomes behaved. As the old chemist

1932

March 1 —
Americans read all about a sensational crime: Famous aviator's baby son, **Charles A. Lindbergh, Jr.,** *is kidnapped and killed.*

May 29 – July 28 —
The Bonus Army. Congress promised WWI soldiers a bonus—in 1945. Thousands of out-of-work veterans and their families march to Washington to ask for their bonus money now. They're refused. **President Hoover** *sends troops to run them out of their makeshift camp. Two veterans are killed in the fiery violence.*

Nov. 8 —
In the presidential election, **Herbert Hoover** *is overwhelmingly defeated by* **Franklin D. Roosevelt** *(FDR) (see 1933).*

A deadly serious business

lay dying in 1943, scientists were getting down to business on the top-secret Manhattan Project. The goal? To make a bomb like no other, one that would end WWII—they hoped. How? Physicist J. Robert Oppenheimer and all of the other scientists would use tools and discoveries that had already been figured out, then experiment, measure, reason, and record their observations, often mathematically. This is the scientific method. Think of it like this:

1933

Adolf Hitler, leader of the Nazis (*National Socialist German Workers Party*), rises to power in Germany.

March 4 —
On his Inauguration Day, **FDR** *names* **Frances Perkins** *as Secretary of Labor, the first woman in a presidential Cabinet.*

March 31 —
Congress passes **FDR's** *idea of a Civilian Conservation Corp. The CCC hires thousands of jobless fellows to work in national forests.* **FDR** *has so many government plans put in place that the first months of his presidency is named the Hundred Days.*

The men and women building the atomic bomb were working with more than government money and Ernest O. Lawrence's cyclotron (see time line, 1930). They were armed with all of known science, created by everyone from Aristotle in ancient Greece to Enrico Fermi in 20th-century Chicago (see time line, 1942).

Would the bomb work? Would the U.S., Great Britain, Russia, and their allies defeat Germany and Japan? George wouldn't find out, not in this world anyway. He peacefully passed away in the evening of January 5, 1943.

George was buried at Tuskegee, not too far from the grave of his old boss, Booker T. Washington. These words were carved on George's tombstone: "He could have added fortune to fame, but caring for neither, he found happiness and honor in being helpful to the world."

Visitors pay their respects to George.

1934

1935

Swiss-born American **Jean Piccard** *goes by hydrogen-filled balloon 57,500 feet into the air to study cosmic rays.*

May 23 — Police gun down notorious bank robbers **Clyde Barrow** *and* **Bonnie Parker.**

Dust storms blacken Midwestern skies, destroy farms, and compound the fearful misery of the Great Depression.

CATCHING THE VISION

SYMPATHY CARDS AND PEOPLE BY THE HUNDREDS poured into Tuskegee. "The world of science has lost one of its most *eminent* (outstanding) figures," Franklin D. Roosevelt wrote in his telegram.

Was the President correct? Yes. George absolutely was and still is one of America's most famous scientists.

"In my opinion," said Henry Ford, talking about his friend in 1942, "Professor Carver has taken Thomas Edison's place as the world's greatest living scientist."

Really? Well, it's good that Mr. Ford was loyal to his friend, but you'd be hard pressed to find a top-10 list of great scientists with George's name on it. An admirable man George genuinely was, but he was sorely lacking in scientific method. If people were working on a top-secret Peanut Project, they'd have trouble finding proven facts and formulas in Dr. Carver's chemistry lab.

1936

1937

Educator **Mary McLeod Bethune** *becomes the first black woman to direct a U.S. Government agency as she heads the Division of Negro Affairs of the National Youth Administration.*

At the Berlin Olympics, German Chancellor **Adolf Hitler** *refuses to present the four gold medals won by black-American track star* **Jesse Owens.**

Walt Disney *and his team make* Snow White and the Seven Dwarfs, *the first full-length animated film.*

"I have all of those formulas," George told an interviewer in 1938, "but I have not written them down yet." He pretty much never did. He researched multitudes of projects, concepts, and products, but it wasn't in his nature to document his findings. Ideas interested him more than facts and figures. So how could other chemists test his work and learn from it? What kind of a scientist was he? And how come George got so much praise? Did he deserve it?

The answers are like the man himself: complicated. How could he not be? Because his brilliant, multi-talented mind came packaged in dark skin in an era when the rights of black people were either trampled or ignored, George had to get past all sorts of barriers. As a kid, he had to take to the road all by himself to get an education. His deep faith, his genuine smarts, and his ambition were all mixed up with his need for recognition. His country's cruel, irrational race problem tangled with George's image of himself and the way others saw him. In a time when there was so much anger and suffering among America's blacks, it suited powerful whites to put soft-spoken George in the spotlight as sort of an honorary member of their race and a credit to his own. It suited him, too. Regardless of

1937

May 6 —
Lakehurst, NJ —
A first: People hear this disaster described on the radio. The Hindenburg, a hydrogen-filled German dirigible (blimp) explodes in flames.

May 27 —
San Francisco, CA —
The 4,200-foot-long Golden Gate Bridge opens for business.

July 2 —
Pacific Ocean —
Aviator **Amelia Earhart** vanishes while flying around the world.

PROFESSOR CARVER'S CARDINAL VIRTUES

He left us with lessons on more than being a good Earth-keeper. On January 9, 1922, in a letter to one of his students, George expressed his hope that "each one of my children will rise to the full height of your possibilities, which means the possession of these eight cardinal virtues which constitutes a lady or a gentlemen."

1st. Be clean both inside and outside.

2nd. Who neither looks up to the rich or down to the poor.

3rd. Who loses, if need be, without squealing.

4th. Who wins without bragging.

5th. Who is always considerate of women, children, and old people.

6th. Who is too brave to lie.

7th. Who is too generous to cheat.

8th. Who takes his share of the world and lets other people have theirs.

1938

1939

June 22 — New York, NY — African-American boxer **Joe Louis** keeps the heavyweight crown when he knocks out his German opponent, **Max Schmeling**.

Oct. 30 — Actor **Orson Welles** turns H. G. Wells's War of the Worlds into a radio play. It sounds so real that loads of listeners believe Martians are invading Earth.

American physicist **John V. Atanasoff** takes the world closer to modern computers with his semi-electronic digital device.

their ethnicity, poor folks who were struggling through hard times found encouragement in the way George climbed so high from so low-down in life. He became famous because of his wisdom, inspiring personality, life story, and his blackness — not because he was a great scientist. He wasn't? No, but he was a great thinker, one who used science and art to help himself and others understand the world.

"Would it surprise you," George once asked a visitor who'd been noticing all of the scientific and artistic things he'd done, "if I say that I have not been doing many different things? All these years I have been doing one thing…seeking Truth. That is what the scientist is seeking. That is what the artist is seeking; his writings, his music, his pictures are just expressions of his soul in his search for Truth."

Henry A. Wallace, who'd known George since his own Iowa boyhood, offered this way of understanding the Peanut Wizard, a.k.a. the Sage of Tuskegee: "Dr. Carver had an insight into the nature of things different from most scientists. He had possibilities of an even greater contribution than most folks realize."

More than anything, George was a teacher. He taught by example how an individual could live with dignity in an unfair

---

1939

It's flickering; it's black-and-white. New York World's Fairgoers see their first program on television. Next year, CBS will show off another techno-breakthrough: television in color.

When **Marian Anderson** is not allowed to sing in a Washington, DC, concert hall because of her color, First Lady **Eleanor Roosevelt** arranges for her to perform at the Lincoln Memorial, where 75,000 people come to listen.

In the U.S., Russian engineer **Igor I. Sikorsky** builds and flies the first practical single-rotor helicopter.

world and how all individuals could practice good Earth-keeping. He was "green" before today's eco-champions were born. Decades ago, he showed folks how to recycle and build up their land naturally instead of using it to death, then standing helpless when soil washed or blew away. He showed how nature and mankind could co-exist in harmony, so Earth was cared for as well as all the people on it — not just a few rich grabbers getting richer, surrounded by poor, hungry multitudes on a burnt-out planet under birdless skies.

In 1896, a slender black fellow sat on a southbound train, thinking how he might teach and help his "people." Sure, George meant his race—people of color—but his vision was large enough for everybody. Could we not all be his people? Are we not all humankind? The lessons he taught are plenty necessary for us all. "The thing that makes me happier than anything else," he wrote not long after he came to Alabama, "is that my own people are catching the vision, I mean the vision of centuries to come."

Catch George's vision. Let this picture play on the theater of your mind: The whole human race living well together on Earth, a blue-green oasis amidst the stars.

1939   1940

Cartoonist **Bob Kane**, 18, invents Batman.	*Sept. 1 —* **Adolf Hitler** *sends German tanks and bombers into Polish territory and pretty much begins World War II.*	*German forces overwhelm Western Europe.*		*July 4 – Sept. 2 — Chicago, IL — To celebrate achievements by blacks in the 75 years since the Emancipation Proclamation, a Diamond Jubilee Exposition is held.*

AND THEN WHAT?

A MONTH AFTER GEORGE DIED, Missouri Senator Harry S. Truman responded to all of the letters he'd been getting and called for an official U.S. park down where George was born. President Roosevelt signed the bill into law on July 14, 1943. The George Washington Carver National Monument was a first for

Moses and Susan's house at the George Washington Carver National Monument

1940

Nov. 5 —
Franklin D. Roosevelt *becomes the first and only President to be elected to a third term.* **Henry A. Wallace** *is FDR's running mate.*

1941

Forest Mars, Sr. *begins selling the candy he's invented: M&M's.*

March 6 —
*Mount Rushmore, SD —
Sculptor* **Gutzon Borglum** *dies of a heart attack before he finishes carving his huge presidential portraits.*

Berlin, Germany

Americans, black or white. Up until then, only Presidents had national parks set aside to honor them. Less than a year later, FDR was reelected to his fourth term in office and that Missouri senator was his Vice President. So it was that Harry S. Truman, 60, became the 33rd President on April 12, 1945, because Franklin D. Roosevelt, 63, died that day at Warm Springs, Georgia. Later that month, 56-year-old Adolf Hitler took his own life in bombed-out Berlin, Germany, a week before his defeated nation surrendered to the Allies on May 7, 1945. Many millions were dead, but WWII *still* wasn't over.

While Allied forces set about liberating Nazi-invaded, bomb-blasted Europe, the war with Japan raged on, all through the

1941

1942

Dec. 7 — Pearl Harbor, HI— Japanese bombers destroy ships, aircraft, and kill or wound some 3,700 people. The next day FDR asks Congress for a declaration of war against Japan.

Aug. 7 — The Solomon Islands — U.S. Marines and soldiers begin six months of brutal fighting for control of Guadalcanal. Far, far from the South Pacific, Russians are suffering and fighting German invaders.

South Pacific Ocean. And those Manhattan Project physicists — remember them? — inched ever closer to test-blasting their invention. On July 16, 1945, near Alamogordo, New Mexico, there was an enormous, expanding flash of green light, roaring and soaring into a mushroom cloud 8,000 feet high. On August 6 and 9, almost 42 years after the Wright brothers' flight, a U.S. plane dropped two atomic bombs, one over Hiroshima, the other over Nagasaki, killing nearly 250,000 Japanese people. Countless thousands more were dreadfully injured, sickened, or homeless. Their government surrendered on September 2, 1945. That was the end of WWII and the beginning of the atomic age, but that's another story — and a troubling one at that.

Hiroshima, Japan

1942

Dec. 2 — Chicago, IL —
In a carefully controlled test, Italian physicist **Enrico Fermi** *and his team make a uranium atom split apart and release energy, causing more splitting, more energy, and so on. This nuclear chain reaction is what makes an atomic bomb explode.*

1943

April 18 — Warsaw, Poland —
Jews battle with Germans invading the part of the city to which they've been confined. The Holocaust (Nazis' extermination of European Jews) is well underway.

Was the atomic bomb a good use of science and scientists? It is a desperately difficult question, but, as George Washington Carver would tell you, that's what science does best. It guides you to a never ending questioning, answering, then more questions, such as what should we do — or not do — with our knowledge? How can we use all that we've discovered to heal the world and make life better? How can we people of Earth explore farther in and away, deeper down, and higher up? George left us some of the answers — and an invitation: "I am not a finisher," he said. "I am a blazer of trails. Little of my work is in books. Others must take up the various trails of truth and carry them on."

Plant.

Learn.

Catch the vision.

1943

Eisenhower

U.S. pilots are bombing Germany. The Japanese are fighting to hold on to South Pacific islands. When will the Allies invade Europe (June 6, 1944) and start pushing the Nazis back to Berlin? Details will be up to **Dwight D. Eisenhower,** the new top general.

1945

May 7 —Germany surrenders. The war in Europe is over. Americans celebrate V-E (Victory in Europe) Day on May 8.

Aug. 14 — Japan surrenders soon after the bombings of Hiroshima (Aug. 6) and Nagasaki (Aug. 9). Official papers will be signed on Sept. 2. World War II is over.

MORE
INFORMATION

G.W. Carver Chronology

1864 or 1865 — George (GWC) is born in Diamond Grove, MO.

1877? – 1880 — He attends school in Neosho, MO, then moves to a series of Kansas towns: Fort Scott, Olathe, Paola, and Minneapolis. During this period of his life, George adopts "Washington" as his middle name.

1884 — GWC studies and works as a clerk in Kansas City, MO.

1886 – 1888 — GWC begins farming near Beeler, KS, completing his sod house on April 18, 1887.

1888? — He gives up his homestead and moves to Winterset, IA.

Sep. 9, 1890 — He enrolls as a student of art and music at Simpson College, Indianola, IA.

1891 – 1894 — GWC earns a Bachelor of Science degree at Iowa State College of Agriculture and Mechanical Arts, Ames, IA. (His foster mother, Susan Carver, 77, dies Jan. 23, 1892.)

1893 — GWC exhibits his art at the Chicago World's Fair.

1894 – 1896 — GWC, graduate student and instructor at Iowa State, earns his Master of Agriculture degree.

Oct. 8, 1896 — GWC becomes Tuskegee Institute's Director of Agriculture.

Dec. 20, 1910 — Moses Carver, George's owner then foster father, dies at age 98.

1916 — GWC is invited to become a Fellow of the Royal Society for the Encouragement of Arts, London.

Jan. 1921 — GWC, lobbying for American peanut growers, appears before the Ways and Means Committee, U.S. House of Representatives, Washington, D.C.

1923 — The NAACP awards its annual Spingarn Medal to GWC.

1928 — Simpson College (IA) awards GWC an honorary Doctor of Science degree. He'll receive an honorary doctorate from Selma University (AL) in 1942 and another one from Iowa State University in 1994.

Feb. 10, 1940 — George Washington Carver Foundation (a.k.a. Carver Research Foundation) is signed into existence.

April 7, 1940 — Booker T. Washington becomes first African American pictured on a U.S. postage stamp.

March 11, 1941 — George Washington Carver Museum is dedicated.

Jan. 5, 1943 — George Washington Carver dies at the Tuskegee Institute.

July 1943 — Congress passes H.R. (House Resolution) 647, creating the GWC National Monument.

1948 — GWC is pictured on a 3¢ U.S. postage stamp. President Harry S. Truman desegregates the U.S. armed forces.

1956 — Simpson College dedicates its Science Building to GWC. (Iowa State will do the same with its Science Building in 1968.)

June 15, 1966 — Nuclear-powered submarine USS *George Washington Carver* is commissioned.

July 2, 1964 — The Civil Rights Act of 1964 is signed into law. All businesses must serve all people regardless of color, race, religion, or national origin. Later this year, Marin Luther King, Jr., leader of black citizens' civil rights movement, is awarded the Nobel Peace Prize. Later this decade (1967), Thurgood Marshall becomes the first African American to serve as a justice on the U.S. Supreme Court.

1985 — The Institute becomes Tuskegee University. Scientists there begin working with NASA (National Aeronautics and Space Administration), researching the soil-less cultivation of sweet potatoes in space, among other things.

1990 — GWC becomes part of the Inventors' Hall of Fame.

1998 — GWC is pictured on a 32¢ U.S. postage stamp.

JAMES WRIGHT invents SILLY PUTTY® *1943* | *1946* **PERCY SPENCER** invents the **MICROWAVE OVEN** | *1947* **Willard F. LIBBY** finds a way to learn the age of prehistoric life forms

1st DVD Players *1996* JARON LANIER pioneers "Virtual reality" *1984* Rob't Kahn & Vint Cerf develop the INTERNET *1983* spacecraft is launched 1st reusable COLUMBIA

SCIENCE & INVENTION MARCH ON

1946
J. Presper Eckert, Jr. & John W. Mauchly build ENIAC, the first fully electronic digital computer. www.seas.upenn.edu/~museum/

1947
William Shockley, Walter Brattain, & John Bardeen invent the transistor. www.pbs.org/transistor/

1951
Marion Donovan invents disposable diapers. www.women-inventors.com

1957
Space race begins with Russia's Sputnik I. history.nasa.gov/sputnik/

1955
Dr. Jonas Salk's new polio vaccine is safe and it works! www.achievement.org/autodoc/page/salobio-1

1953
Francis Crick, Rosalind Franklin, & James Watson discover the structure of molecular, genetic building blocks: DNA (deoxyribonucleic acid). www.pbs.org/wgbh/nova/photo51/

1964
Douglas Engelbart invents the computer mouse. www.ibiblio.org/pioneers/englebart.html

1969
A first for humans: **Neil Armstrong** walks on the moon. http://starchild.gsfc.nasa.gov/docs/StarChild/whos_who_level2/armstrong.html

1st permanent artificial is implanted in a patient. *1981* U.S. spacecraft VIKING I speeds off to planet MARS. *1975*

with radioactive **CARBON 14** | **1952**  1st **Diet SODA** | **1959** **JACK KILBY** and **ROBERT NOYCE** invent the **microchip.** | **Ruth HANDLER** invents the **BARBIE**®doll.

1997
Only ewe: A sheep is successfully cloned.
www.sciencemuseum
.org.uk/antenna/dolly/
index.asp

1991
The World Wide Web is invented.
www.w3.org/People/
Berners-Lee/

1990
The Hubble Space Telescope is launched.
www.hubblesite.org

1965

James T. Russell | **1966** Jerry D. Merryman, JACK KILBY, & James H. Van Tassel invent the compact invents the FIRST hand-held CALCULATOR. disk.

2001
Dean Kamen *develops the Segway.*
www.dekaresearch.com

1978
Louise Brown, *the first test-tube baby (conceived outside of the mother's body) is born.*
http://news.bbc.co.uk/
2/hi/health/3093429.stm

2007
Norman E. Borlaug *leads worldwide agricultural research.*
www.worldfoodprize.org

1976–1981
The rise of the personal computer.
www.pbs.org/nerds/
timeline/
www.computerhistory
.org/timeline/

1970
April 21: Folks call attention to their planet's plight.
www.earthday.net

1967 JOCELYN BELL discovers

(computer assisted tomography.) | **1970** | PULSARS | (neutron stars)
Godfrey N. Hounsfield and Allan M. Cormack are developing CAT scan technology

RESOURCES FOR YOUNG SCIENTISTS AND INVENTORS

http://www.nationalgeographic.com/science

National Geographic Science & Space site lets you
explore the solar system, see how the human body works,
go inside Earth, and much more in this fact-packed site.

www.usfirst.org

This site is home of FIRST (For Inspiration and Recognition of Science
and Technology). Inventor, businessman Dean Kamen founded it in 1989 so he
could rev up young people's excitement about science and technology.

http://sciencespot.net/Pages/kdzinvent.html

Very accessible!

http://www.sallyridescience.com/

Sally Ride was the first American woman to travel in space (1983),
but you'll find LOTS more than star stuff at this cool site.

http://starchild.gsfc.nasa.gov/docs/StarChild/StarChild.html

Got your head in the stars? Check out this NASA site.

http://kids.yahoo.com/science

A very cool reference source.

http://dmoz.org/Kids_and_Teens/School_Time/Science/

This site is totally loaded with informative links plus homework help.

http://kids.nypl.org/science/inventions.cfm

I especially like the time line links
on this site.

http://www.clpgh.org/kids/homework/subjectlinks_inventions.html

Check out this one. You'll find lots of info here.

AUTHOR'S RESOURCES

BIBLIOGRAPHY

Burchard, Peter Duncan. *George Washington Carver: For His Time and Ours.*
National Park Service, 2005.

Herries, Meirion & Susie. *The Last Days of Innocence: America At War, 1917–1918.*
New York: Random House, 1997.

Horton, James Oliver, et. al. Editors. *A History of the African American People.*
New York: Smithmark Publishers, 1995.

Kremer, Gary R., Editor. *George Washington Carver: In His Own Words.*
Columbia, MO: University of Missouri Press, 1987.

McMurry, Linda O. *George Washington Carver: Scientist and Symbol.*
New York: Oxford University Press, 1981.

Newhouse, Elizabeth L., et. al. Editors. *Inventors and Discoverers: Changing our World.*
Washington, D.C.: National Geographic, 1988.

Wilkinson, Philip and Michael Pollard. *Scientists Who Changed the World.*
New York: Chelsea House Publishers, 1994.

PLACES WELL WORTH VISITING

George Washington Carver National Monument
5646 Carver Road, Diamond, MO 64840
417.325.4151
http://www.nps.gov/gwca

Tuskegee Institute National Historic Site
1212 West Montgomery Road
Tuskegee, Alabama 36088
334-727-3200
http://www.nps.gov/tuin

THE PICTURES

As artists have for centuries, I scribble out my pictures with a pencil.
I go over the pencil drawing with ink, using India ink and a sharp steel nib that's been
pressed into a wooden or plastic penholder then I erase all of the pencil lines.
With white paint, pencil, and black watercolor, I'll fuss with the details and shading.
And as for those details, I study pictures in many a reference book
to make sure they are correct. The illustrations are drawn
at the size you see in this book— very picky!

THE WORDS

I didn't start writing about GWC because I was an expert on the man,
but, rather, because I was curious about him. GWC himself wrote of his early life
in autobiographical essays reprinted in G. R. Kremer's book, noted in
Author's Resources. I read what he wrote and said, but I needed to know more.
What did folks say about him? What was going on in his time in the world?
I learned and could report to you what I found out, thanks to the work of
historians, journalists, photographers, and biographers.
I learned about George, a great man well worth knowing.

INDEX

ACKNOWLEDGMENTS
I wish to thank Park Ranger Curtis Gregory of the GWC National Monument
and the rest of the knowledgeable personnel at GWC's historic sites.
They caught the vision.
To my niece Katie Harness, who went with me to Tuskegee, Alabama,
and to writer-friend Veda Boyd Jones, fellow traveler to
Diamond, Missouri, I dedicate this book.

Book design by David M. Seager. Design production by Ruthie Thompson, Thunderhill Graphics.
Text and display type are set in Celestia Antiqua.

For information about special discounts for bulk purchases, please contact
National Geographic Books Special Sales: ngspecsales@ngs.org

For rights or permissions inquiries, please contact
National Geographic Books Subsidiary Rights:
ngbookrights@ngs.org

Library of Congress Cataloging-in-Publication Data

Harness, Cheryl.
The groundbreaking, chance-taking life of George Washington Carver and
science & invention in America / by Cheryl Harness.
p. cm. — (Cheryl Harness histories)
Includes bibliographical references and index.
ISBN 978-1-4263-0196-4 (hardcover, trade)
ISBN 978-1-4263-0197-1 (hardcover, library)
1. Carver, George Washington, 1864?–1943.
2. Agriculturists—United States—Biography.
3. African American agriculturists—Biography. I. Title.
S417.C3H28 2008
630.92–dc22
[B]
2007029316

Printed in the United States of America

Founded in 1888, the National Geographic Society is one of the largest nonprofit
scientific and educational organizations in the world.
It reaches more than 285 million people worldwide each month through its
official journal, NATIONAL GEOGRAPHIC, and its four other magazines;
the National Geographic Channel; television documentaries; radio programs;
films; books; videos and DVDs; maps; and interactive media.
National Geographic has funded more than 8,000 scientific research projects
and supports an education program combating geographic illiteracy.

For more information, please call 1-800-NGS LINE (647-5463)
or write to the following address:
National Geographic Society, 1145 17th Street N.W., Washington, D.C. 20036-4688 U.S.A.
Visit us online at www.nationalgeographic.com/books.